Children's Talk in Communities and Classrooms

Understanding Children's Worlds
General Editor   Judy Dunn

The study of children's development can have a profound influence on how children are brought up, cared for, and educated. The central aim of this series is to encourage developmental psychologists to set out the findings and the implications of their research for others – teachers, doctors, social workers, students – who are responsible for caring for and teaching children and their families. It aims not to offer simple prescriptive advice to other professionals, but to make important innovative research accessible to them.

Children's Talk in Communities and Classrooms

Lynne Vernon-Feagans

BLACKWELL
Publishers

Copyright © Lynne Vernon-Feagans, 1996

The right of Lynne Vernon-Feagans to be identified as author of this work has been asserted in accordance with the Copyright, Designs and Patents Act 1988.

First published 1996
2 4 6 8 10 9 7 5 3 2 1

Blackwell Publishers Inc.
238 Main Street
Cambridge, Massachusetts 02142
USA

Blackwell Publishers Ltd
108 Cowley Road
Oxford OX4 1JF
UK

Library of Congress Cataloging-in-Publication Data
Vernon-Feagans, Lynne.
    Children's talk in communities and classrooms / Lynne Vernon-Feagans.
      p.   cm. — (Understanding children's worlds)
    Includes bibliographical references and index.
    ISBN 1–55786–482–9 (hbk. : alk. paper). — ISBN 1–55786–483–7
(pbk. : alk. paper).
    1. Afro-American children—Education (Elementary)—North Carolina—
Case studies. 2. Marginality, Social—North Carolina—Case
studies. 3. Poor children—Education (Elementary)—North Carolina—
Case studies. I. Title. II. Series.
LC2771.VA7 1996
871.97′96′073—dc20   96–1119
                                                  CIP

British Library Cataloguing in Publication Data
A CIP catalogue record for this book is available from the British Library.

Typeset in 11 on 13 pt Sabon
by Graphicraft Typesetters Ltd, Hong Kong
Printed and bound in Great Britain by Hartnolls Limited, Bodmin, Cornwall

This book is printed on acid-free paper

To all the children and families
who so graciously allowed us
into their lives

Contents

Series Editor's Preface

When they first start school, children face a whole series of new demands and expectations, and a new social world. We would surely all agree that this is a potentially important transition for them. Indeed, it is now known that problems in adjustment to those first years of school can cast a long shadow. The question of which children are most at risk for difficulties in starting school is clearly of real social importance, as is the issue of what can be done to help them. In the USA, children take this step into another world when they are five years old, and they take it from families and communities that differ dramatically in cultural and economic terms. As Lynne Vernon-Feagans points out in this book, the public educational system in the USA – available to all children – is regarded as a place of opportunity for all. The hope is that here in the public schools, all children – regardless of their economic, cultural, and ethnic backgrounds – will have access to the best education possible. School, as she notes, is supposed to be the great equalizer. Yet it is clear that children from economically disadvantaged backgrounds, and from minority ethnic groups, are at much greater risk for educational and social problems at school than children from more affluent, White families. What features of their family and community lives and their experiences at school are key to their difficulties?

Lynne Vernon-Feagans' research examines these issues through a study of the experiences of two groups of children beginning school: a group of poor African American children in semi-rural North Carolina (half of whom had been in an intervention program since birth), and a comparison group of White children. The focus of the book is upon the children's talk as they played in their home communities and in the classroom, on their interactions with their teachers, and on interviews with family members, community leaders, and teachers. Through the evidence of the children's conversations in their neighborhoods, Dr Vernon-Feagans hopes to dispel some of the damaging myths about the quality of such children's language, and about their families and communities. Through her detailed analysis of teacher–pupil conversations in kindergarten and second grade she highlights the implications of teachers' practices, showing for instance how teachers' practice varies with high- and low-ability groups, and with children from the two groups she compares.

The lessons from the research for those concerned with the education of children growing up in poverty and discrimination have significance not only for the USA, but world-wide. There are encouraging messages as well as disappointments in the story; children who received the preschool intervention, for instance, were doing better on measures of IQ, language use, and achievement at school – but attempts to provide intervention at school age were not successful. And the gap between the African American children and those in the other group widened as the children grew up. The challenges that the book presents for those concerned with the education of children, for those involved in policy decisions about preschool provision, are all too clear, and unquestionably important. The conversations and narratives of the children in the study vividly portray the experiences of the children as they made the transition to school. To clarify the developmental implications of such real-world experiences at home and at school is a central goal of the series *Understanding Children's Worlds* in which this book appears.

Preface

Children are not in any way expendable. They are God's choicest vessels, his greatest treasures, and ours as well. The greatest responsibility we have is the care and nurture of children: No other moral responsibility exceeds this one. And yet we know to our great sadness that children are an endangered species. It is not that there are too few of them. It is that we do not take care of the children and do not regard them as assets. . . . We must recover the sense of urgency that says that children are the only real treasure we produce.

Peter J. Gomes, 1993, p. 28

Children in the United States enter public school at 5 years of age to begin what is generally considered the most important context for their future well-being as adults. Although the age at which children enter school varies from country to country around the world, almost every community and almost every family looks to the publicly financed educational system as the place where their children will develop the skills needed to contribute to their home community and the wider society. Although this public educational system is available to all children in the United States and most industrialized countries and is supposed to be the great equalizer among people, a place of opportunity for both the most and the least privileged among us, in reality, the beginning of school has become an insidious way to segregate many among us who do not fit into the mainstream of the culture, even as we profess to help all children obtain the best education possible.

Although this book is about a group of poor African American children in the United States, half of whom participated in an early daycare intervention program and half of whom did not, their experience of the transition to public school at age 5 is probably not unique to the United States. Poverty and ethnic diversity among children are current or emerging issues in many industrialized countries. Many of these children fail to adjust and learn in mainstream school settings despite the efforts of the larger society to provide what is considered an "appropriate educational environment" in school. This book provides a description of these children's lives as they enter school and explores some of the possible explanations for the children's failure. Some ways to prevent this failure are also suggested, based on the data gathered about the children, their families, and the schools.

The book is arranged into eight chapters. Chapter 1 outlines the purpose of the study of these children's lives and provides both a theoretical and a historical framework within which to interpret the data presented about the children and their families. Particularly important is a description of how early education for low-income children developed in the United States and how our study contributed to learning the "how, when, and why" of early intervention for children living in poverty. Chapter 2 describes the families, communities, and schools that provided the children's support during the transition to public school. This information was obtained through interviews with families, visits to neighborhoods, and observations and talks with teachers in classrooms. Chapter 3 describes the philosophy behind the early intervention project and describes in detail the curriculum objectives and the overall structure of the intervention effort. In hindsight, the strengths and weaknesses of the intervention are also discussed. Chapter 4 provides data about the lives of the children in their home neighborhoods as they make the transition to school, by analyzing their talk with peers and adults during play times after school. These data are presented both quantitatively and qualitatively to paint a broader and richer picture of the children's lives outside of school. Chapter 5 examines the experience of the children in classroom small group activities, directed by the teacher. These so-called "ability groups" are the core of instruction where teachers introduce new concepts, especially for the teaching of reading. Chapter 6 presents data from a structured teacher–child book-reading tutorial that we constructed to try to mimic teaching situations in the classroom setting. Chapter 7 contains information on other aspects of the children's school experiences, especially with regard to the effectiveness of the early intervention in school success. Data from standardized tests and questionnaires through elementary school are described. Finally, chapter 8 tries to provide some solutions for the educational community so they might better teach children whose poverty or ethnicity have been barriers to success in traditional mainstream school settings.

But before the study is described in detail, it might be helpful to provide a brief introduction to the education of poor and minority children, using the United States as an example. In the melting pot of the regular public school classroom in the United States or elsewhere, there are a variety of ethnic groups and children with a variety of disabilities. This diversity in the classroom has heightened the awareness of the individual differences among children and the need to individualize instruction to address these differences. The language used in the desegregation orders of the 1960s in the United States and in the laws protecting all children with disabilities in the 1970s mandated that children from all backgrounds and abilities be afforded a free and appropriate education in the least restrictive and most integrated environment. This last phrase has been interpreted as education for all children in the mainstream public school classroom with children who are in the "mainstream" of the culture. The philosophy and rhetoric that ushered in many of the new laws protecting children who were members of minority groups and/or who had some disability should have created a more equitable and gentler educational system that accepted and even celebrated the differences among children. Yet the enormity of the task of mainstreaming children was not really envisioned by the policy-makers. Change in the law was mandated, but a change in how the culture at large viewed the differences among children and how to teach these children could, unfortunately, not be mandated. A similar situation is found in England, where immigrant children have presented challenges to the educational system (Tizard et al., 1988).

In order to accomplish these mandates for equality of education for all children in the United States, the educational system has responded to the minority populations by integration of the schools using forced bussing, redistricting, and the creation of large magnet schools to replace smaller and less efficient neighborhood schools. To accomplish the assimilation of children with a variety of special mental or physical disabilities, mainstreaming these children into the regular classroom environment has been implemented. These mandated changes have required the development of teaching specialists to help the already overburdened regular classroom teacher, who has been generally unprepared for such changes. The proliferation of specialists has heightened the awareness of differences among children both to the benefit and the detriment of children. On the one hand, specialist teachers have helped children with disabilities assimilate into the mainstream of education and they have helped children from different ethnic backgrounds to assimilate to the language and/or dialect of the mainstream. On the other hand, the very act of the recognition of these differences has often led to unintentional labeling of these children as less ready to benefit from the "regular" classroom experience of mainstream middle-class children. This recognition has appeared to segregate some children from others as many overburdened regular classroom teachers abrogated their responsibility for these children, relegating their special needs to the "special" teachers. In the process, these changes have often resulted in the unintended poorer overall adjustment to school for children with learning problems and children from minority groups. All this benevolence in the name of individualizing instruction has too often led to the discrimination that the laws were meant to eliminate.

In many ways the schools of thirty or even one hundred years ago in the United States were actually more accepting of the differences among children. In the days of the one-room schoolhouse, the teacher was expected to teach everyone at every grade level. It often happened that older, more competent children became the actual teachers for the younger, less competent children. Teachers clearly knew there were individual differences in aptitude for learning, but these differences were blurred in a classroom with children of different ages and backgrounds. The purpose of the educational endeavor was to prepare the children to participate productively in the life of their home community. This did not mean that all children learned to read well or learned to work with numbers, but it generally meant that children found a path through school that would lead them at some point into becoming a meaningful part of the community. This positive aspect of schooling has generally often been lost in today's schools in America, where it may be difficult to define "community" and where families and teachers do not live close to each other, and where family mobility forces children to change schools and communities often over the school years.

The other way in which these schools of years ago were more appropriate for non-mainstream children was the community involvement in schools. In the years when the United States was a more rural and small-town country, communities truly owned their schools, with the educational establishment part of the fabric of the community. Teachers lived in the town where they taught. They personally knew the families of the children they taught. They knew the children outside of school, in church and synagogue, and in community activities. Teachers saw the families of the children informally, and in this way valuable information was exchanged between families and the school. Children knew that their education in the classroom was linked inextricably to the life of the community, so that schools in rural farming towns were fundamentally different from the schools in industrialized factory towns. The schools reflected the needs and values of the community they represented.

With the advent of the "modern" era of schooling have come magnet schools, state-mandated curricula, integration, specialized teachers, and much more. This has happened not only because of the economics of efficiency but because the advent of technology has created the need for specialty teachers and specialty information that large and mandated curricula can accomplish so well. These "modern" changes have occurred in other industrialized countries as well. It has also happened in order to accomplish mandated integration of children from minority groups. Only by some form of bussing and rezoning of school districts was it possible to balance schools racially, since housing patterns in the United States have not generally been ethnically diverse. Ethnic minorities, like the majority population, often chose and still choose to live together even when the opportunity is provided for them to live in more ethnically diverse areas. This has resulted in a decline in the community involvement of ethnically balanced schools, especially by minority families. In the rush to integrate schools and provide specialized education for all, there was a lack of awareness of the vital importance of the community investment in the schooling process. The ownership by home communities of these new kinds of schools has been accorded much less importance than the more surface restructuring within our schools.

Although today we are certainly better at understanding the individual differences among children, we have not progressed very far in meeting the needs of these differences so that these differences do not divide our children but unite them. We have not been able to address the individual needs of children and still make them feel an integral and equitable part of the mainstream. The laws have not been able to help us much in accomplishing the humanitarian mission of equality and access to the best education for all children.

This book is the story of the transition to school of a group of poor African American children in a fairly small, progressive Southern town in the United States; however, the issues are likely to be representative of children living in poverty in many industrialized countries of the world. These children were not yet a part of the mainstream of the culture and the school system was struggling to try to educate these children in the best way it knew, given the needs and constraints imposed upon the schools by the larger society. Thus this study reflects the struggles in this rather small community as well as the larger society in trying to address the inequities created by discrimination and poverty. The group of African American children in this study were identified as "at risk" for school failure. This risk status reflected the history of discrimination against Black

Americans in the United States. In addition, like too many African American children in this country, these children were also living in poverty. Fortunately, at the time of our study, unlike many children living in poverty, few of these children were exposed to the crime and violence that now plague most of America's large cities. These were children of families who did not move North or to large cities and the families were proud to say so. Their "risk status" was clearly rooted in those experiences of poverty and discrimination that come inextricably bound together because of the history of the treatment of Black Americans in the United States and elsewhere.

The initial purpose of the study was to examine the language of the children in their home community and the schools, but as we collected the data for the study, we realized that these data revealed much more about the culture of the community and school as well as the values and attitudes of the larger society that helped shape both our mainstream and African American children. As this story unfolds, it has some parts missing. Although we have talk by children in their home communities and classrooms, we have missed talk in the actual home setting itself, on the playgrounds at school, and in the churches and other important community settings that influence children and families. We have tried to fill in these missing parts by interviewing family members, community leaders, teachers, and informants who so graciously agreed to help us shape parts of this story. In the final analysis it was the children themselves who told us their story of the transition to school, and we owe it to them and all our children to listen to their words carefully.

Acknowledgments

Thanking all the people and agencies who have been responsible for this book would be impossible, especially given the breadth of such a project and the length of time many people have been associated with it. Hopefully, I will acknowledge at least some of the many who made this project possible. Its major funders were NICHHD and the Spencer Foundation, both in the United States. A small grant from the Center for the Study of Child and Adolescent Development at the Pennsylvania State University helped with the writing of this book.

Thanks must first go to my co-investigators whose vision of this project helped at its inception and through data collection. Ron Haskins was the creator of the family interview and the one who allowed me to use the data to paint a more accurate portrait of the families and their lives. He was also my partner on many excursions to the neighborhoods of the children, always willing to romp through woods and fields helping me gather the language samples with the tape recorder strapped to my or his back. Dale Farran helped design and carry out the studies in the classrooms with teachers and children. Without her persistence we could never have completed the data collection in so many places at the same time. She played a key role in the development of the initial coding systems of the large corpus of language samples from the classrooms and the tutorial sessions.

There were at least four critical people at the Frank Porter Graham Child Development Center who initiated this project and kept it going over the years. James Gallagher was the Director of the Center during the major portion of this study and his support was crucial to its success, along with the Associate Director, Craig Ramey, who created the idea, design, and name for this study. Two individuals who held this project together on a day-to-day basis for 20 years and who have given me feedback on the many drafts of this book deserve particular recognition, for without their dedication the project could never have been carried out successfully. They are Carrie Bynum and Francis Campbell.

There are many others to thank also. The cooperation of the school administrators and teachers was critical to gathering our data and to understanding the many competing demands faced by teachers in diverse classrooms. In addition, there are those who helped in data preparation, collection, and analysis. Some of them are: Susan East, Debbie Jeffreys, Mary Ann Kimball, Paul Yoder, Ella Akin, Tom Richey, Chuck Burnett, Kaye Fendt, Neal Finkelstein, Margaret Morris, Marie Butts, and Gina Walker.

Special thanks go to Judy Dunn for her careful comments on several drafts of the book, and both Linda Burton and Richard Lerner who commented on parts of the book relevant to their interests. The preparation and editing of the manuscript were expertly accomplished by Teresa Charmbury, making my task so much easier.

Last, thanks go to my family who were there when I needed them. I appreciate the good thoughts and deeds of my three children, Brian, Laura, and Robert, and the moral support of my husband, Jock Lauterer. Thanks to his memory of a photographic assignment in 1969, he was able to find wonderful pictures that he took of the same homes and communities described in this book. These photos have contributed immeasurably to a more vivid description of the home environments of the children.

Figure 7.1 is reproduced from Campbell, F., and Ramey, C. (1994). Effects of early intervention on intellectual and academic achievement: A follow-up study of children from low-income families. *Child Development*, 2, 684–98.

Every effort has been made to trace copyright holders. The publishers apologize for any errors or omissions, and would be grateful to be notified of any corrections that should be incorporated in the next edition or reprint of this book.

1

Poverty, Language, and Early Intervention

It is universally recognized that when children come to school, there is a wide gap between those who are best prepared and those who are least prepared for school learning. The question then is how to close the gap early, for if it is not soon closed it will widen. This is the way with gaps of such kind.

Donaldson, 1978, p. 98

Language as a Focal Point

Although there are many skills that young children acquire, the one that seems almost magical in its emergence is children's rapid acquisition of language. Children from different backgrounds and with exposure to very different language environments acquire the rudiments of language in the first two or three years of life. The acquisition of this language system can be described as the separate and interlocking learning of four major components of language. First, children learn to use the specific sound system that is particular to their native language (phonology). Second, they learn the rules that govern the way words are strung together to make a sentence (syntax), such as those that form active versus passive sentences. They learn many different words and their meanings in the third component (semantics). And last, and most important for this study, children learn how to use language in context (pragmatics). This last skill not only involves acquisition of the first three components but is intertwined with knowledge about the social and cultural network of the larger environment in which the children live. The use of language by children in a variety of contexts will be the focus of this study.

Scholars such as Jean Piaget (1926), interested in the cognitive development of children, have especially been interested in studying language as a window into children's minds. Vygotsky (1978) also described the language of children as a manifestation of human consciousness and thought. More recently language has also been seen as a way to characterize children's social development by examining how children use their basic language skills to interact with others. Dunn (1988) has argued that young children can use language in sophisticated ways that demonstrate their awareness of the feelings of others as well as their strategies in managing complex relationships with others.

In this book we will examine children's talk in a variety of situations during the transition to public school. Not only will we be interested in the content of dialogues in which children engage at home and in school, but we will be most interested in describing children's use of language strategies during the learning of culturally valued activities in their home community and how these same strategies may be adapted to negotiate children's learning in school. The description of the Black children's transition to school is really a story of how their culture and learning style are reflected in their talk both in their home community and in school. The response to this style of language and learning by both mainstream teachers and children also reveals the sometimes subtle differences in style that can lead to major miscommunication and misattribution of intention by the mainstream culture about Black children's overall competence in school.

Since this study involved African American children, some might mistakenly think this means a study of Black Dialect. But we mean much more than the surface features of language divorced from context and culture. Our study will examine both a broader and a deeper use of language including the beliefs in the culture about language and the cultural traditions and activities that shape the use of language in conversation with others and in storytelling. By examining children's talk in the culture of the home and the neighborhood where the children live, we can have a better understanding of how the cultural use of language affects the transition to school and how an early intervention program might help that transition.

In order to place this study in the context of the larger issues in Western society with respect to schooling of minority and poor children, and to understand the particular interpretations offered to explain our results, both a conceptual and a historical overview can help to clarify the story that emerges from our analyses of the children's talk during the transition to school. This also provides an opportunity to explore how schooling is viewed in the example of American culture, and especially how it is viewed with respect to the assimilation of minority groups.

A Conceptual Framework: Four Perspectives on Development and Learning

Four complementary perspectives can be adopted to describe the overall framework employed to examine the language used by children and adults in their home community and at school. The first is what has been called a developmental/contextual perspective, that emphasizes the importance of examining the different settings in which individuals participate so as to understand the reciprocal processes of the individuals within each context as well as the continuities and discontinuities among the different contexts for individuals across time. This perspective also provides evidence for the importance of individual differences in development and how these differences have implications for understanding different pathways during critical developmental transitions, such as the transition to school.

The second perspective focuses on children's participation in the culturally valued activities that form the fabric of their lives. The focus of development shifts from the individual in settings to the processes that affect the way information about the culture is transmitted from the expert to the novice within these valued activities. This perspective takes seriously not only contextual differences but also sociocultural differences between and among societies and may help to explain different learning styles among different cultures and ethnic groups.

The third perspective examines the specific nature of social exchanges between individuals and the mechanisms that control reciprocity and synchrony within relationships. In addition, this perspective provides some framework for the development of overall skill in maintaining and changing the social interactions of children with peers and adults.

The fourth perspective deals specifically with racism in the United States and how the larger society has prevented African Americans from sharing in the prosperity of the country through a series of invisible institutional barriers. Ogbu (1991) has articulated this castelike status of African Americans, especially as it relates to ways in which public schools are structured in the United States and the systematic discrimination against minorities through the schooling process.

These four perspectives have not emerged from the language research literature but were conceived to understand how culture and context affect the development of children. They lend themselves more clearly to the purposes of this book than perspectives on basic language development because our interest is in how children use their language in a variety of settings that are important for development.

A Developmental/Contextual Perspective

For many years developmental psychologists have acknowledged tacitly the importance of context in development. This context notion has been conceived in a molar way by Valsiner (1989), in his conceptualization of the cultural context for development. A more microsetting conceptualization of home and school has been described by Barker (1963) and Bronfenbrenner (1979). These authors have argued that the individual's behavior, as well as the interpretation of that behavior, varies from context to context and from culture to culture. Behavior that is measured outside of the naturally occurring context, for instance in a laboratory, is viewed with suspicion unless there is good reason to argue that the individuals will perform naturally in such an unnatural setting. This contextualism has taken a number of different forms that emphasize the importance of the different aspects of the settings, including the physical and psychological characteristics that influence the behavior of the participants in each of their many naturalistic settings.

One of the first environmental (contextual) psychologists was Barker (1963). He argued years ago that these different behavior settings for development contained different demands for behavior that could dramatically affect the behavior of the individuals in that setting. One of his major contributions was to carefully describe the balance that exists between the demands that must be met for a setting to operate effectively and the number and skill level of the individuals participating in that setting. For instance, his contrast between overmanned and undermanned behavior settings gave rise to a better understanding of the psychological differences between large and small schools. In the setting of a small as well as a large school there are similar demands for one football team, one class president, and one yearbook editor. These demands need to be met, no matter how many or how few children attend that school. Settings that have few people to meet the demands required by the setting are called undermanned behavior settings; those that have too many are called overmanned behavior settings. In a small school, children usually are compelled to fill many roles in order to fulfill the demands for the setting or activity. Thus, even marginally competent children perform important functions like cheerleader, basketball player, yearbook editor, etc., because these roles must be filled if the activity within the setting is to be accomplished. Children in these undermanned behavior settings are often able to take on roles that they might never have had an opportunity to explore in a larger, more overmanned setting. Evidence suggests that this forced participation and responsibility actually enhances the self-esteem of these children. On the other hand, in large schools, many children, especially less competent and less assertive children, are less likely to perform important roles in the school because the setting does not demand roles for all of its children. It has been argued that the children who are not needed in the overmanned setting feel marginalized, have lower self-esteem, and often perform less well in the school setting. The movement among large schools to create schools within schools has been partially motivated by this contextual work.

In the present study we are concerned about the context of home and school and the subcontexts within these major settings. The contrast between the language behavior seen at home and at school can be seen as a function of the demand characteristics of each setting and the language skills that the children bring to that setting.

Children bring to settings certain personal characteristics that are reacted to by the setting and the people in it. Depending on how well the child's skills and personal characteristics fit the demands of the setting, positive or negative feedback will be given to the child by the setting. Each time the child enters this same setting, it is likely that the child's characteristics will be reacted to similarly and in fact might escalate over time. This continual feedback and escalation has been called a feedback loop by Lerner (1984). These positive or negative feedback loops can continue over time to produce either enhanced or hindered development. For instance, a child with a high physical activity level may receive positive feedback from parents and neighbors if he/she lives on a farm where his/her high activity level can be channeled into the many physically demanding activities of the farm; but this same high activity attribute may receive negative feedback for the child living in a one-room apartment in New York City or in a classroom where sitting at one's desk for long periods of time is highly valued. Lerner (1984) emphasizes the individual differences among children and their "goodness of fit" with the different settings they inhabit. Thus, "fit" characterizes the way in which the individual characteristics are accepted and enhanced within the setting. In this framework, a child might have a good fit in one setting and a less good one in another. Returning again to Barker, a smaller school setting has a greater tolerance for "fit" because the needs of the setting demand that roles be filled even if there is not a perfect fit. Larger schools can be more selective and have a tighter window for "goodness of fit" because of the large number of children available to participate in any one setting. In this way many of our schools can marginalize children who do not fit the ideal characteristics of the setting.

Bronfenbrenner (1979) has schematized in a more systematic way the kind of settings that influence children. Children participate as members in microsystems, such as home, school, and neighborhood. Important to Bronfenbrenner and to the study here are the transition and links between one microsystem and the next (mesosystems). The system of links between settings is important for the transition from one to another. A child can make a smoother transition between home and school if the parents and teachers form communication links that can facilitate the understanding of the child in one setting and the next. Natural mesosystem links can be created when one microsystem contains similar demands and activities as another microsystem. For instance, middle-class or mainstream parents often try to create activities at home, such as workbook activities, reading together, and desk work, that mimic activities at school.

If a child participates in two microsystems that have very different demands, this can create difficulties for the child's smooth transition between them. Thus a child may look quite competent in one setting and incompetent in the other. Behavior that is adaptive in one setting may not be in another. Strong mesosystem links are even more critical when the demands in the different microsystems are not the same. The active child who may adapt well in the home setting may need parents who help create facilitative mesosystems or links to school, where high activity level is generally not tolerated. Communication between home and school may allow the very active child to make the best fit possible in the classroom setting. This emphasis on the importance of the major influence of context on understanding the continuities and discontinuities in behavior form the basis of much of this book.

The Cultural Context of Participation

The views of contextualism discussed above characterize the unique and the different contexts in which the individual functions. Although these formulations have been useful in mapping out the different levels of context important for development, those perspectives have not focussed on the differing cultural value placed on one context as compared to another or the activities of the setting that define the value of the context for each cultural or ethnic group. Rogoff (1990) presents a multicultural focus and also tries to make the interaction among people in context as the unit of analysis, rather than each individual or the context itself. In her view, the child's development is defined within many of the culturally valued activities of the community. These activities are those that define the competent adult. In a Mayan village, this might constitute the ability to hunt, cook, and weave beautiful cloth. In mainstream America it may constitute being a lawyer, doctor, housewife, or teacher. The activities related to becoming competent in these roles constitute highly valued cultural activities. In the Mayan village competence is achieved through guided participation. Children observe and gradually participate in these activities, such as weaving. There is no one there to judge failure; all children succeed through gradual participation and guidance by a more skilled person, either an adult or an older child. Rogoff calls this the apprenticeship model, one in which both the expert and the novice benefit from the participation and where failure is not emphasized because the expert's job is to gradually allow the novice success in small steps until competence is achieved.

In mainstream America many valued activities in the home and community setting are similar to those in the Mayan village. Parents use the apprenticeship model for teaching children how to repair the car, cook, entertain friends, and so on. Scouting and other activities in the community use the apprenticeship model for learning camping, hiking, and other valued group-oriented activities. Unfortunately, most schools in America and elsewhere in Western culture do not use the apprenticeship model any longer. The one-room schoolhouse often made use of experts and novices working together to create competence, but in our "major" industrial schools of today, with same-age segregation and same-skill segregation the norm, the opportunities and value of apprenticeship in learning have drastically diminished.

This guided participation perspective calls for attention not only to the understanding of the skills needed at home or in school but also to those valued and frequent activities that might naturally be learned by novices through guided participation in an apprenticeship relationship. For instance, Schieffelin (1979) found that adults in Papua New Guinea rarely talked to young infants and children during culturally important activities and that young children were often excluded from interaction with adults. It was older siblings and peers who taught infants early language and social interactive skills.

In mainstream Western culture emphasis has been placed on studying the mother, who has been seen as the one who teaches the young infant interactive skills. This is reflected by the hundreds of studies which have examined early mother–child interaction and communicative development in mainstream middle-class children, but this is probably not the case in other ethnic groups within the United States.

Like Vygotsky, Rogoff believes that cognitive development is fostered through interaction with others, and in Rogoff's view this is centered around social activities, such as joint bookreading in middle-class America and weaving in a Mayan community. For Rogoff, the unit to examine is not the child but the totality of the activity and how the activity contributes to development. The activity itself is the developmental process, not the individual elements. We will try to examine some of these culturally valued activities for our children.

Synchrony and Reciprocity in Interaction

The ethological approach as represented by Cairns (1979) helps to identify those mechanisms that maintain interactions, resulting in a description of maneuvers by the players in the interaction that creates a delicate balancing act. Cairns emphasizes the evolution of synchrony and reciprocity during the young child's early interactions with others. Synchrony refers to interactions that provide mutual support, so that one person's actions are coordinated with and supportive of the others. These interactions need not be between equals. Mothers and babies are often seen in synchronous interactions because the mother adjusts her behavior to support and coordinate with the infant. Reciprocity occurs "when the acts of two or more persons support each other in a relationship and their actions become similar to each other" (Cairns, 1979, p. 296). Reciprocity is one kind of synchrony when the activities and emotions of the participants are similar. Not all synchronous and reciprocal activities are positive. For instance if one child hits another, a reciprocal action by the other of hitting back can escalate into a very negative interaction. Thus, in some cases it is an asynchronous activity that can actually sustain an interaction. If one child hits the other and the recipient of the hit responds asynchronously by trying to talk about why the other child hit him/her, then the result could be the maintenance of the interaction and resolution of the conflict. These children have developed quite sophisticated synchronous and reciprocal strategies during interaction that maintain effective interaction, especially during culturally valued activities in their home communities.

Changes in the mechanisms of social interaction can result in developmental advances for the child. These are often seen first not in the laboratory situation but in naturally occurring relationships where the child can demonstrate the highest levels of interactive style, as with family members in familiar settings. These developments may be characterized as nonreciprocity and escape from synchrony, according to Cairns (1979):

> Perhaps the problem of social development is not to achieve synchrony – that is assured in early infancy – but to escape from its constraints. Failure to match one's responses to another's and the ability to select alternative pathways that do not escalate in intensity, become significant accomplishments for the person as he or she approaches maturity. To achieve consistency, the child must be able at some points to escape the boundaries of reciprocity. (p. 308)

Patterns of interaction tend to become consolidated over time with repeated occurrence of similar cues to elicit the sequence and patterns of behavior. Thus these patterns of synchrony and asynchrony tend to change somewhat depending on context, but consolidation is a powerful force that may produce functional behavior in one setting and dysfunctional behavior in another.

For the present study aspects from all these views of development in context will be taken into consideration, but particular attention will be paid to the cultural activities that are valued at home and at school and to how the home and the school may differ for the groups of children examined. Thus an attempt will be made to expound on Rogoff's conception to characterize the culturally valued activities for the groups of children in their home community and the way in which guided participation is structured there in contrast to the guided participation in school. By examining the way in which the interactions are consolidated through repetitions and how these consolidations differ by context and cultural group, we can better understand why some children have either an easier or a more difficult time in the transition to school.

Prejudice, Discrimination, and the Castelike Status of Minorities

Although the children in this study were selected for early intervention because of their background of poverty, all but one were African American. This confound between ethnicity and poverty creates the imperative to interpret our findings in light of the history of prejudice and discrimination against Black Americans as well as to more carefully examine the values and beliefs of our families.

A number of recent scholars have distinguished between overt and covert intentional discrimination (Hill, 1991; Cheatham, 1991). Overt discrimination refers to institutional laws and restrictions that prevent certain groups of individuals from participating in certain activities. Overt discrimination is easier both to understand and to change. The laws of the late 1970s and after to protect the rights of minorities have eliminated most of the overt discrimination in American culture. Covert discrimination refers to more subtle ways in which individuals from minority groups are excluded from participation. This kind of discrimination is insidious and more difficult to eradicate. For instance, tracking children in school into ability groups for instruction will almost inevitably ensure, because of the confound between race and poverty, that African Americans will be overrepresented in the lower ability groups or tracks in school. Children in lower ability groups have been shown to receive less complex and important instruction (Goodlad, 1984).

Ogbu (1982, 1991) has argued convincingly that schools, in particular, create structural barriers so that Black Americans lead a castelike existence, being excluded from participation in the mainstream society of school by virtue of race. Although our study was not designed to systematically examine the subtle aspects of racism in America, the data reported here certainly confirm the subtle covert racism that pervades our public schools and this perspective will be used in the interpretation of our findings of the children's views about school and their experience in the classrooms.

Schooling, Ethnicity, and Poverty

According to Valsiner (1989), formal schooling has two major functions in society. First, it transmits basic knowledge and skills that are not usually available in the home or neighborhood setting. Second, it inculcates the values and beliefs of the dominant cultures, often promoting loyalty to ideological systems that are not always coincident with those of the child's family group. It has not always been acknowledged that schools play this second role, and in fact many educators have tried to make schools "culture-free" havens where knowledge is acquired unburdened by cultural baggage. For instance, the National Commission on Excellence in Education in the United States called for a back-to-the-basics movement, an increase in discipline and an increase in testing the objective knowledge of students (Linney & Seidman, 1989), free of cultural bias. On the other hand, the *Turning points* document from the Carnegie Corporation (1989) emphasized the concept of schooling, making education touch the important values we hold, and using these important values as a touchstone for learning.

Trying to deny that culture permeates our transmission of knowledge in schools is rather futile, since there is really no way that the structure of our schools and the teachers who teach can deny the cultural traditions and beliefs of the larger society. For instance, in Japan the classrooms contain many more children than American classrooms do. One teacher instructs 50 to 60 children with much enthusiasm and dedication.

In fact, when asked about the large numbers in the classes, teachers responded that it would be bad for children to be in small classes since they need to learn how to manage their lives in large groups (Lewis, 1984). This surely would not be the response given by teachers in the United States where there is implicit emphasis on the individual and on individualized instruction. Teachers in the United States have pushed for smaller classes so that each child can maximize his/her potential, reflecting the views of the larger society that puts the individual, not the group, at the center of learning.

There is no universally right or wrong way to structure schools, but certainly some ways are more synergistic with the society they represent than others. Culture then becomes a rather elusive vapor that creeps into all we do. It is important to try to illuminate certain aspects of the dominant culture that may be a barrier for those coming from different, but just as legitimate, cultural traditions.

All over the world literate societies and cultures generally begin this formal schooling of children at between 5 and 7 years of age. Although this universal schooling purports to serve children from many different backgrounds and with different ability levels, it is clear that many of our world's children fail in our formal educational system. In American culture, this failure usually begins early and becomes worse over the elementary school years (Entwisle & Alexander, 1990). In studies done 20 or 30 years earlier, it was found that children's long-term school achievement was set in the first few years of formal schooling (Bloom, 1964; Kellam, Ensminger, & Turner, 1977). A more recent study reported similar findings (Alexander & Entwisle, 1988) in the early school experience of Black and White children in Baltimore. In general, those children who were members of minority groups or poverty groups, and those with some special learning problems, did more poorly in school even if they began school on the same intellectual footing as their non-risk counterparts.

The combination of poverty and minority status has been particularly devastating in the United States, with national statistics revealing that these children have more than double the dropout rate and grade retention than other children (National

Commission on Children, 1991). Since more than 20 percent of children in the United States are growing up in poverty, and this group contains a disproportionate number of minority children, this failure of the educational system to serve these children has an enormous societal cost in lost potential for these children and great financial cost to society in the form of joblessness, criminality, and many of the other problems associated with poverty. For instance, 80 percent of incarcerated persons in the United States are high school dropouts (Committee for Economic Development, 1991).

The reasons for this failure are clearly complex in any society but may be particularly difficult to understand in a multicultural society like that of the United States, where many different ethnic groups have contributed to the cultural values and practices of the mainstream society, including minority groups that have been discriminated against for generations. Our multicultural society is at great risk of not addressing the needs of all of its citizens, and especially its children, without a concerted effort to understand and incorporate the beliefs and cultural traditions of these minorities into the schooling process. Ogbu (1988; 1991) has forcefully argued that in the United States, minorities – especially African American minorities – have been systematically excluded from mainstream education. The "caste-like" status of these groups, he argued, created a system where the belief in having what the majority White population had was unattainable. The consequence was the development of an alternate system of how to "make it" in society. The system, which contained beliefs and practices that helped these minorities accept their position in society, usually rejected the traditional educational system. Part of the story we will tell in this book will try to describe some of these alternate systems for young African American children. As Ogbu (1991) has argued about African American minorities:

> In their folk theory of "making it" involuntary minorities often wish they could advance through education and ability as white Americans do, but know they cannot. They come to realize that it requires more than education and effort to overcome the barriers set up against them. Consequently, they develop a folk theory

of getting ahead which differs from that of white Americans.
(p. 153)

Ogbu's castelike perspective also postulated that the majority group interpreted the behavior and beliefs of the minority groups in a negative way so that the "victim was blamed." A version of Ogbu's position on minority children has been incorporated into the rhetoric of a recent United States review of the status of its children (National Commission on Children, 1991). The National Commission that wrote the document recognized that for some ethnic and cultural groups school achievement held few tangible rewards, and "for many children and their parents, assimilation meant rejecting their own cultural background in order to reap the benefits of mainstream society" (National Commission on Children, p. 184). In a study in England, this same perspective was used to explain poor and minority children's failure in school (Tizard, Blatchford, Burke, Farquhar, & Plewis, 1988). The English schools did not value minority cultural backgrounds and the different ways the children approached the learning process. According to the authors, the children began to do poorly in school and were then blamed for their failure because of their ethnicity.

Ogbu's perspective, as well as that of others interested in the strengths of the Black family (Cheatham & Stewart, 1991; Spencer, 1985; Spencer, Brookins, & Allen, 1985), helps to place the results of our study in the present multicultural milieu of today's children in the United States. In order to understand the nature of this study of children's transition to school it is necessary to look at the historical issues that have led up to the present study and the social context in which it took place. A knowledge of this historical perspective is important in order to understand the limitations of the early intervention program described here, as well as to understand the way the public school experience affected our children's response to schooling.

The "Deficit Hypothesis"

The recent emphasis on dominant versus minority cultural conflict is in contrast to the original explanations for the school failure of poor and minority groups that prevailed in the 1960s. The prevailing view at that time focussed on the deprivation of experiences that characterized the home lives of poor and minority children and their families in comparison to the "ideal" mainstream children and families. This 1960s view had a monolithic flavor that masked the large individual differences among poor families as well as the cultural and ethnic beliefs and practices that had little or nothing to do with "deficiencies." Although it has always been clear that children reared in poverty have had fewer opportunities while away from the school environment to participate in school-like experiences at a young age, this did not mean that they were deprived of complex learning situations that required high levels of reasoning and language ability. Unfortunately, the original research in the 1960s did not focus on the home and neighborhood contexts of these children where opportunities for such complex reasoning indeed did occur.

The original research and review articles on school failure of minority and poor children characterized children reared in poverty as having an impoverished environment which led to the children being ill prepared for the cognitive demands of school (Bereiter & Engelmann, 1966; Bernstein, 1971; Hess & Shipman, 1965; Rutter, Yule, Morton, & Bagley, 1975). These studies particularly targeted language as an area of deficiency in these children. Deficiencies in language included assuming that dialect differences implied poor grammar and vocabulary, making these children appear less verbally sophisticated. This less sophisticated language was often postulated as the cause for these children's school failure. This view has generally been discarded as more culturally balanced interpretations have been provided, but the large mainstream culture still harbors negative views of poor children. Tizard et al. (1988) conducted a study in England of inner-city minority children and interpreted the problems the children had in a very different way than had the researchers of the 1960s. She explained the previous interpretations of the data this way:

> The great majority of white researchers have assumed that the cause of underachievement, insofar as it is not explained by social

class, is located in the "problem" of children of Afro-Caribbean origin and their families. This assumption is clearly shown by the fact that they have chosen to investigate factors in the child and the home and not teachers and school processes. During the sixties and seventies the children's failure to progress was widely blamed on their own characteristics, especially their use of Creole and their negative self image, although by the end of this period both these explanations were much less frequently heard. This is because research showed that children of Afro-Caribbean origin born in Britain are likely to have a reasonable command of the syntax of standard English, as well as a form of Creole. They appear able to switch from one code to another, and the great majority do not have difficulties in reading or writing arising from the influence of Creole. (p. 11)

The original work examining social class and ethnic differences in language was motivated by the good intentions of scholars who wanted to help these children succeed in society, but by using the word "deficit" the interpretation inevitably led to false attributions about these children and their families. Researchers and educators were trying to discover why poor and minority children did so poorly when they entered public school, with the underlying assumption that the problem resided within the child, not the school or larger society. Studies done in the 1960s (Bereiter & Engelmann, 1966; Bernstein, 1961; Deutsch, Katz, & Jensen, 1968; Raph, 1965) characterized the language of low-income and/or minority children as underdeveloped. These children performed more poorly on vocabulary tests, produced fewer words, and were generally less effective in communicative situations. The inference made from these results was that the low-income and minority children were exposed at home to a less verbally stimulating environment that led to less verbal ability and school competence in these children.

One of the initial exponents of this deficit theory was Basil Bernstein (1966; 1971) whose hypotheses were based on social class differences in England. He tried to characterize the differences between middle-class and lower-class children's language in an attempt to help explain why lower-class children did not do well in school. He coined the terms "elaborated code" and "restricted code" to characterize the language of these children. Children from lower-class families in England were said to have a "restricted code" for language. This style of language consisted of using simpler, less complex sentences, with fewer subordinate clauses, greater use of pronouns, especially with no clear linguistic referent, and the use of high frequency common words. This "restricted code" relied on nonverbal means of communication more than the "elaborated code." According to Bernstein, this less sophisticated code was available to all children but only children from middle-class families had access to an "elaborated code" of language. This code was characterized by complex sentences, explicit reference, and a more sophisticated and creative use of language with less reliance on nonverbal communication.

Bernstein's characterization of children in England greatly influenced work in the United States. Many studies quickly appeared in American journals, using such terms as "cultural deprivation" and "verbal deprivation" to describe the early verbal experiences in the homes of poor African American children. One of the most famous of these language studies was reported in a book called *Teaching disadvantaged children in the preschool* (Bereiter & Engelmann, 1966). These authors took a very extreme position, arguing that poor and minority children were almost devoid of language interaction skills, and proposed "teaching" children how to talk. Their ideas had some initial acceptance as preschool programs adopted some of the behavioral techniques suggested, but overall the book disappointed most of the research community because of the clear misinterpretation of "cultural and dialect differences," as demonstrated in this paragraph:

> The speech of the severely deprived children seems to consist not of distinct words, as does the speech of middle class children of the same age, but rather of whole phrases or sentences that function like giant words. That is to say, these "giant word" units cannot be taken apart by the child and re-combined; they cannot be transformed from statements to questions, from imperatives to declaratives, and so on. (p. 34)

The source of these differences in language between middle-class and lower-class children was thought to reside not only within the child but within the family, especially the behavior of the mother. A number of studies (Deutsch, Katz, & Jensen, 1968) led by the work of Hess and Shipman (1965; 1967) examined how low- and middle-income mothers interacted with their children, especially focusing on the mother's use of language in interaction with her child in structured teaching tasks. They and others found that low-income mothers used more imperatives, more nonverbal responses, fewer utterances in answering questions, and poorer strategies in helping their children solve problems in a teaching situation. These data were all collected in a university research laboratory setting. Hess and Shipman (1967) concluded that the teaching styles and information obtained from the family (almost always the mother) "set limits upon the potential mental growth of the child unless an intervention program was instituted" (p. 103). Their strong interpretive statements about the environmental input provided by these low-income mothers gave rise to an entire area of research still active today that places the mother as the central figure in the child's environment and maintains that she is the one who contributes in a major way to her child's language and cognitive development. Hess and Shipman's (1967) view of the child's deficits centered on the deprivation of environmental input that was often verbal in nature. They state:

> The meaning of deprivation would thus seem to be a deprivation of meaning in the early cognitive relationships between mother and child. This environment produces a child who relates to authority rather than to rationale, who may often be compliant but is not reflective in his behavior, and for whom the consequences of an act are largely considered in terms of immediate punishment or reward rather than future effects and long-term goals. (p. 103)

The Early Intervention Solution

The concern about the impoverished environments of poor children and the possible detrimental effects of these environments on the children's development occurred during an era in the United States when there was optimism about the possibilities for rapid change in the environment that would quickly eradicate poverty and other social ills. The political phrases of the day, including "War on Poverty" and "The Great Society," ushered in the era of possibility for all peoples.

There was an equally optimistic view of change in developmental psychology and education. J. McV. Hunt's book *Intelligence and experience* (1961) helped change the way scholars had been thinking about intelligence and cognition. Hunt argued that intelligence was not fixed and that there was evidence that the interaction between genes and environment could produce permanent positive change, especially if the environment was enriched in the early years of life when change was most possible (Hunt, 1961). He concluded that "it is no longer unreasonable to consider that it might be feasible to discover ways to govern the encounters that children have with their environments, especially during the early years of their development, to achieve a substantially faster rate of intellectual development and a substantially higher adult level of intellectual capacity" (p. 363). The work of Hunt and others influenced policy-makers who saw the opportunity to make large-scale changes in the poor and minority populations in the United States.

The kinds of interventions proposed for young poor children were diverse, and ranged from the then popular behavioral approaches in the preschool years, such as the Bereiter and Engelmann program (1966), to the more Piagetian approaches (Weikert, Roger, Adcock, & McClelland, 1971), to the more family-oriented and social/cognitive approaches of Caldwell (1968) and Gray and Klaus (1968). Although at the time these programs were innovative and diverse in perspective, they all focussed attention on the child or on the child and family, trying to enhance language through direct instruction or through teaching the mother new strategies of interaction with her child.

These kinds of approaches proved somewhat successful and some of these programs have had long-term positive effects on the children and the families (Lazar et al., 1982). Yet, the approaches were limited because it was assumed that what was best for every child was what was seen in "middle-class," mainstream families. Our intervention for low-income children in North Carolina was begun at the end of this period when there was optimism about the plasticity in development in the early years of life; it included some unique elements, reflecting this optimism, that will be discussed in a later chapter. Suffice it to say that our project began with great hopes that our intervention could radically change the life trajectories of our children by placing them in a daycare intervention program.

In addition to the smaller demonstration and research projects funded by the federal government, quite revolutionary social programs also emerged during this optimistic period in history. The largest and most well known of these social programs for children was the Head Start program that began in 1965. Lyndon B. Johnson announced its beginning with the hope of the prevention of school failure and the subsequent cure for future poverty in the United States. Although Johnson spoke of teachers using new approaches for teaching poor children, the focus was on preparing the children for school, not for preparing teachers to deal with the children. Johnson's words were:

> We have taken up the challenge of poverty and we don't intend to lose generations of our children to this enemy of the human race . . . But today . . . children who have never spoken learned to talk. Parents who were suspicious of school authorities came to see the centers and they stayed on to help the teachers. Teachers tried new approaches and learned new techniques. (Johnson, 1965, *New York Times*)

Some of this rhetoric was reminiscent of the interpretation of the language performance of poor and minority children described by Bernstein (1966) and Bereiter and Engelmann (1966), but there was some emphasis given to parents and teachers as well. These Head Start programs had differential success, as will be discussed later, but ultimately the ones that were successful in the long term were successful not because the children "learned to talk" or because they acquired new skills, but because the designers of Head Start had the foresight to envision a community-based intervention, using teachers and parents in partnership to help children make the transition to school. Thus, although it was an intervention program that focussed efforts on the children, not the schools, it contained the seeds of a successful program with its innovative cultural and home community curricula.

The Head Start programs around the country differed in many ways, especially in the length of time children were able to attend. Some programs were year-round and began when the children were 3 years of age, while others began in the summer months prior to the children entering kindergarten. There was much excitement about the Head Start program. The orientation of the programs differed but all seemed to include the families and be centered in the communities where the children lived.

Disillusionment with Early Intervention

The effects of these Head Start programs were initially thought to be quite impressive, but the infamous Westinghouse report (1969) revealed that the intelligence (IQ) advantage for the children attending these programs was rather modest and that the advantage disappeared in the first few years of elementary school. The ensuing debate about this evaluation centered around the narrowness of the outcome measures, namely IQ. Although the Head Start programs were aimed at improving cognitive skills measured by IQ, the broader goal was to help these children adapt to school and to become productive members of society.

The debate over the effects of early intervention was further fueled by an article that appeared in the *Harvard Educational Review* in 1969, by Arthur Jensen. The article argued that the short-term IQ gains by the early intervention program participants were doomed to be short lived because intelligence was fixed and could only be temporarily increased by environmental manipulation. The provocative opening statement in his article exclaimed: "Compensatory education has been tried and it apparently has failed." Not only did Jensen argue that compensatory education had failed; he also implied that the differences in IQ among the racial groups was fixed because these differences could not be explained on the basis of environmental variation. His basic argument was that the environment acted as a threshold variable. If a child was exposed to extreme environmental deprivation, he argued, the child might not perform at her or his genetic potential, and yet an enriched preschool program could not boost the child above his or her fixed potential. In his view the most influential environmental variables occurred prenatally and were likely to be nutritionally and/or biologically based.

The response to Jensen's article was swift and angry. A supplement of the *Harvard Educational Review* challenged many of his assumptions and conclusions. Kagan's rebuttal (1969) typified the kind of response that came from many child development researchers. His response to Jensen, titled "Inadequate Evidence and Illogical Conclusions," argued that early intervention programs had not had enough time to be effective, since most consisted only of an eight-week summer program before kindergarten entry, and that at this point it was not known what kinds of programs might be most effective. Many others fueled this debate, which raged into the 1970s and reemerged in the United States in the 1990s with the popular press reporting a similar type of poor reasoning about early intervention in the book *The bell curve* (Herrnstein & Murray, 1994).

The initial response by the federal government to the criticism of early intervention and Head Start was to fund a number of intensive but different preschool programs around the country to see when and if these preschool programs could be effective in helping poor children in America prepare for school. Thus, in addition to the Head Start monies a number of long-term intervention programs were begun in the 1970s.

One of these early intervention programs was the Abecedarian Project which began in 1972. I became a partner in the project in 1976. Although the children and the project will be described more thoroughly in later chapters, it is important at this point to keep in mind the context in which the project began. This particular project ran from 1972 and is still continuing in some form as the oldest children from the project enter early adulthood and the youngest are in junior high school. The Abecedarian Project was conceptualized during a period of intense debate about the effects of early intervention for children reared in poverty, but an era in which money was available from the federal government for large-scale intervention projects like the one to be described in this book. The children in this project were in a daycare intervention project from approximately 3 months of age to school entry at 5 years of age. All elements of their development were scrutinized carefully over the preschool years. A project like this would be very unlikely to be funded today in an era of much less optimism about change.

The Debunking of the Deficit Hypothesis: Language Use Differences

During the 1970s the word "deficit" was finally stricken from the vocabulary of most researchers studying poor and/or minority children, partly in reaction to Jensen but also because of the civil rights movement of the 1960s which helped enlighten the country to the subtle and not so subtle racism and classism that had been so much a part of our society.

The term "language deficits" was purged from the literature on African American children, especially after the work of the linguist William Labov (1969, 1972), who attacked the "deficit hypothesis" with respect to Black Dialect. Not only did Labov argue that dialect was rule-governed and clearly did not connote a deficit, he also demonstrated that the language used on the streets of Philadelphia by young African American boys could be as complex and creative as any, even though these same boys spoke little in the school context.

Labov's seminal work on language in the inner city was extremely important and led to a number of programs in the 1970s that were aimed at helping African American children learn to code-switch, that is, to speak and read Standard English in school while still valuing their own Black Dialect in the home and neighborhood. The programs were also geared toward regular classroom teachers to help them understand the complexities of the rules that governed the Black Dialect the children used in their talk. Clearly, these programs were important but again they were aimed at only a surface manifestation of language (dialect) and they were aimed primarily toward the child, not the family or the structure of the school. The hope was that African American children could somehow succeed in school when the teachers understood Black Dialect and the students could switch from Standard English to Black Dialect over the early school years. Again, of course, these high hopes were dashed. Just because the dialect problem was "solved" did not mean that teachers and schools understood the different way language was used by the African American culture, and it did not mean that other cultural and societal barriers to success could be overcome by an understanding of dialect differences. The minority and poor children were still failing in school.

By the late 1970s research had documented many differences linked to social class and ethnic differences in language (Blank, Rose, & Berlin, 1978; Tough, 1982). These differences captured much more than the superficial grammatical and lexical differences between dialects. There was now a clear emphasis on trying to understand language use differences that dealt not so much with words or grammar but with the use of language in everyday conversations and in narratives in the home and community.

In one of the first language use studies, Blank (1975) compared well- versus poor-functioning African American children in New York City. She found that poor-functioning 12-year-old children answered "why" questions like 5-year-old well-functioning children. In her study children were shown a balance scale and how it worked. After they had understood its purpose, they were asked a series of fairly easy problem-solving questions like "What will happen to the balance when a clip is added?" and then, "Why did that happen?" Although the poor-functioning children did fairly well on the prediction part of the question, they did not do well on the "why" part of the questioning. This was probably because the children did not have experience with interactions that contained "why" questions. In addition, almost twice as many of the poor-functioning children answered the "why" question with an irrelevant response like "My friend can do it." This kind of "unteachable response" made it doubly difficult for these children because teachers were not taught how to respond to such irrelevant answers. Teachers expect children to understand that a causal explanation is required from a "why" question, but children who do not have experience with this kind of question/answer format can face problems in school because teachers may wrongly believe that not being able to answer correctly reflects an underlying incompetence in the children's use of language.

Recently, evidence has accumulated that many of these "poor" answers to "why" questions merely underscored the different cultural "rules" linked to language use. Unfortunately for many minority children, many of these language differences have been misconstrued by the mainstream culture as deficit, not difference, even in today's schools.

The kind of language use demanded in the classroom is actually highly stylized and often quite different from the use of language in children's home communities. This is especially true for low-income and/or minority children. Sinclair and Coulthard's (1975) book, *Towards an analysis of discourse,* described lessons in classrooms in England and actually proposed the structure for language interaction in the classroom. This book, like others of this type, described the sequence of language moves by the teacher and the rules for appropriate responding by the children. For instance, many statements and questions by teachers were actually to be interpreted by children as a command for action. Children who did not interpret the message in this way could incur the anger or disdain of the teacher who might assume that the children were defying her message. For instance, if the teacher said any of the three utterances listed below, especially accompanied by pointing in the direction of the door, she would usually imply by her utterance that the children should interpret her message as a command for action:

1. Michael, do you see the door is open?
2. Michael, the door is open.
3. Michael, would you like to shut the door?

Children who did not interpret these utterances in the way the teacher intended, and just looked up at her in a puzzled way, might find that the teacher inferred a negative motivation on their part, or at the very least poor language comprehension by the children.

It was unlikely that many teachers realized that children were not accustomed to indirect commands like this in the home setting. Cultural differences in the interpretation of seemingly clear situations can be difficult to discern by even the best intentioned teacher. The above example of Michael and the door was quite simple, but in a later chapter more complex examples of the different ways of interpreting the same utterance or series of utterances will be given. Much will be said about larger units of language use, like stories, games, and instructional units. Suffice it to say here that the language research literature in the late 1970s began to become more sophisticated about the complexity of language use and about the complex sets of rules that exist in cultures to interpret the intent and meaning of language in context. This kind of research on language required a real knowledge of the implicit rules of the culture in different settings. This allowed the larger community of educators to introspect a bit more about the implicit expectations of children as they entered school. Although many of these studies documented variations in how different cultural and ethnic groups interpreted the same overt message, most of the studies were not done in the school setting and only speculated on the influence these differences might have on children's school performance.

It was not until the 1980s that a series of studies examined whether the differences between social or ethnic groups in language use could account in any significant way for the school failure of young children, as well as whether these differences were in conflict with the cultural practices and beliefs of the mainstream public schools (Feagans & Farran, 1982; Heath, 1983; Tizard & Hughes, 1984; Tizard et al., 1988). The many studies all seemed to agree, at some level, that most low-income and minority children had different experiences in the home setting compared to middle-class (mainstream) White children, but the studies also found that these home experiences were just as complex and rich in content. Most researchers argued that the home experiences were not capitalized on by the school and that there were real conflicts between the way language was used in the home and the way it was used in school. Tizard and Hughes (1984) presented examples of teachers who were insensitive to the language use of young girls from working-class homes. In one poignant example, a teacher used the Socratic method to try to assess a young girl's understanding of a science project (p. 191). The girl answered only a few of the questions posed by the teacher and her responses were given with some hesitation. The teacher dominated the interaction sequence in such a way that it was clear she did not believe the young girl was capable of answering the questions adequately. This kind of teaching strategy did not stimulate this reticent child to think. The extended talk by the teacher was not the kind of exchange that this working-class child responded to enthusiastically and merely reinforced the girl's feelings of failure in school.

Heath (1983), based on her observations in the home communities of African American poor children in the United States, instituted an intervention program for teachers so they became more sensitive to the cultural backgrounds of their students. She recounted wonderful examples of teachers in small towns in the Piedmont area of North Carolina who were able to capitalize on the cultural differences among children and to excite them about what they were learning in the process. She showed teachers how to encourage children to be participant observers of the language use in their homes and communities, and how to use the information gathered by the children to help the teachers themselves see the continuities and discontinuities between home and school.

The 1990s have seen an emphasis placed on changing the educational system itself to accommodate the growing number of ethnic minorities in the United States. In fact, it is estimated that Caucasians will be a minority of those entering public school by the year 2000. Multicultural education has become an important aspect of most education programs at American universities but it is often devoid of the real content that could specifically help teachers in a multicultural, multi-ability setting. Hopefully this book will give some insight for better teaching, so that assimilation to school can be successful for all of our children.

Summary

This chapter introduced both the conceptual framework to help interpret the data to be presented in the following chapters and a brief historical perspective of the interrelationship among poverty, ethnicity, language, and schooling. This background information should be helpful in placing in perspective the study to be described.

There were four perspectives that guided the conceptual framework, the collection, coding, and interpretation of the data presented. The Developmental/Contextual perspective emphasized the importance of understanding the critical periods in a child's and family's life and also grounded the development of the child and family in context. This perspective underscored the critical influence of the different environmental contexts, such as home and school, on the child's developing self. Our study will carefully examine some of these important contexts for the child's development.

The second perspective complemented the first by adding the influence of ethnicity/culture in context. Rogoff proposed that culturally important contexts where adult and child were together learning culturally important activities created optimal teaching/learning situations. In this apprenticeship model, as Rogoff described it, adults' skills are gradually acquired with no sense of failure by children during the learning process. This atmosphere of teaching/learning has often been found in activities like cooking, fixing the car, or other out-of-school activities. Rogoff suggested that many school-like tasks might be acquired through this model if introduced as an alternate method of teaching many academic skills.

The third perspective focused on the actual system of interaction among individuals in particular settings. This perspective offered a way to interpret the dialogues that occur between children or between adult and child, with respect to the reciprocal or non-reciprocal nature of the talk.

The fourth perspective recognized both the confound between ethnicity and poverty in the United States and the influence of racial discrimination on the development of minority children in this country and others. Institutional racism was not directly measured in this study but the recognition of its influence will be important in the interpretation of the data.

The other major issue addressed was the interplay among factors related to poverty, ethnicity, language, and school adjustment/success. Children of minority status who are also poor have generally been less successful in mainstream schools in Western societies. Various programs have been instituted at the preschool and school-age levels to try to ensure the success of these children. An overview of the literature from the 1960s onward suggested that some of these programs in the United States have been successful but many have been misguided in their attempts. Initial efforts tried to remediate hypothesized "deficits" in poor minority children. Both the "deficit hypothesis" and traditional early intervention programs were changed in the 1970s and 1980s. Currently, there has been a rethinking about the appropriate way to address inequities within risk groups and debate about what is best is still present. With this background in place the next chapters will lay out the design of the study, describe the data collection, and attempt possible interpretations of the information gathered.

2

The Communities, Families, and Schools

The most important work to help our children is done quietly – in our homes and neighborhoods, our parishes and community organizations. No government can love a child and no policy can substitute for a family's care, but clearly families can be helped or hurt in their irreplaceable roles. Government can either support or undermine families as they cope with the moral, social, and economic stresses of caring for children ... The undeniable fact is that our children's future is shaped both by the values of their parents and the policies of our nation.
Pastoral Letter, National Conference of Catholic Bishops, 1991; p. 80 of Wright Edelman, 1992

The adults in our churches and community made children feel valued and important. They took time and paid attention to us. They struggled to find ways to keep us busy. And while life was often hard and resources scarce, we always knew who we were and that the measure of our worth was inside our heads and hearts and not outside in our possessions or on our backs ... that being poor was no excuse for not achieving; and that extra intellectual and material gifts brought with them the privilege and responsibility of sharing with others less fortunate. In sum, we learned that service is the rent we pay for living. It is the very purpose of life and not something you do in your spare time.
Wright Edelman, 1992, pp. 5–6

The approximately 100 children that we had the privilege of following from birth onwards were part of a comprehensive early daycare intervention project for children at risk for later school failure because of the limited economic and educational attainment of their families. Almost all the children were low-income African American children in a semirural area of North Carolina. They entered our project over a period of almost six years and entered public school from the late 1970s through the mid-1980s. The children have been referred to as the Abecedarian Project children. Abecedarian was the name given to the project by Craig Ramey in an attempt to capture the nature of the study, since the word "Abecedarian" means learning from the beginning. At its inception, we the researchers were attempting to carefully document the children's learning and development throughout their childhood as a function of their participation in an early daycare intervention program. Half the children were part of the intervention and half were not, but we tried to carefully follow the lives of all of the children. As the project unfolded it became clear to all of us that we were the Abecedarians and that we probably learned much more from the children and families than they learned from us.

This learning by the researchers was especially apparent in the first few years of the project when most of us had little experience or training in describing the lives of poor and/or African American children. We researchers had mostly come from middle-class families and were educated in traditional developmental or educational psychology programs that, at that time in the 1970s, did not prepare us very well to understand the lives of these kinds of families. We did, though, have a healthy respect for the power of careful observation and assessment which led the project staff to collect an enormous amount of data on the children and their families. As we became more sophisticated observers and interpreters, these carefully collected data became an indispensable reservoir of information in understanding the effects of the intervention and the life trajectories of the children and their families. The evolving interpretation of these children's transition to school involved scrutiny of data on the families, communities, and schools, woven together to try to portray the families, communities, and schools accurately.

It was often easy to mischaracterize the home communities in which these children lived because the quantitative information about the material resources available to the families often misled us into thinking that poverty produces a monolithic experience for children. Observing and talking with the families in their home communities helped us to dispel many of the myths and unwarranted assumptions we held about families who lived in poverty. An understanding of how these families thought about their community and about their children's future, especially in school, helped to create the context to better interpret our data about how the children managed to maneuver through the educational system. Most of the data in this chapter were gathered through observations and interviews with the families and their children as the Abecedarian children entered public school kindergarten.

As the families and communities are described, reference will also be made to two other groups of children and their families that were studied in much less depth at particular time periods during the course of the study. One group of children was selected from the same classrooms as the Abecedarian children. As each of the Abecedarian children entered kindergarten a child of the same sex was randomly selected as a comparison child for the Abecedarian child. This group was more clearly a mainstream group of children, coming chiefly from middle to upper-middle income families because the predominance of children came from affluent families in University Town. These comparison Mainstream children and their families were also interviewed when the children were 5 years of age and were observed and tested during kindergarten. Because we were unable to control the classroom assignments of the children in our sample, different comparison children were chosen each year our Abecedarian children were in school.

A second group was a white low-income group matched on income and parental education with the Abecedarian group. We called these children the Alamance group, the name of the county from which many of these families were drawn. The Alamance families were also interviewed when the children were 5 years of age. There were only 17 families interviewed and only about 30 children tested. Reference to the Alamance group will be made only when they differ from the Abecedarian group.

Before describing the data on the children themselves and their lives in school, this chapter will focus on the communities and homes of both the Abecedarian and Mainstream children, describing data collected in the preschool years and kindergarten. Interviews with the families at the beginning of the children's entry to public school also help to weave the pattern of the children's lives outside of school.

The Home Communities of the Abecedarian Children

The description of the communities where our children lived paints a quite different picture from the one typical of children living in poverty in large cities. Most of the families who participated in the Abecedarian Project were originally from Milltown, which was a small and an almost exclusively Black community until integration in the mid- to late 1960s. This town was a satellite of the White affluent University Town that dominated the economics of the area. In the first half of the century the Black families lived in Milltown or on surrounding farms owned by the Black community. Most of the homes were single-family dwellings and, until recently, many of the families owned their own homes. By the late 1960s and 1970s low-income housing projects were erected in the more White-dominated areas of the more affluent University Town. These pockets of low-income housing projects were initially very attractive and some of our families moved from Milltown to these project homes. Other Abecedarian families lived in houses in Milltown, or in trailers that were often located on a nearby family farm. Most of these farms were small and had one central house, but kin were often allowed to stay in smaller homes or to park their trailer on part of the land.

Table 2.1 presents a portrait of the housing patterns of the Abecedarian families in comparison to the more middle-class Mainstream group, based on our interviews when the children entered public school at age 5. Because of the general affluence of

Table 2.1   Family Housing Patterns (Child Age 5)

		Abecedarian (n = 91)	Mainstream (n = 70)
Ever lived in public housing (yes)		40.22%	2.86%
No. of different homes since birth of Target Child	M (SD)	3.07 (1.81)	3.10 (1.76)
Type of current residence (%)			
home		55.13	80.00
apartment in house		3.85	1.54
apartment complex		30.77	12.31
trailer		8.47	6.15
other		1.28	0.00
No. of rooms in current home	M (SD)	6.02 (1.14)	8.13 (2.27)

the area, the Mainstream children represented the more middle-class nature of the University Town. These children were 90 percent White and were representative of the kind of public school classmates the Abecedarian children encountered each school day.

As can be seen in table 2.1, only 40 percent of the Abecedarian families had ever lived in public housing; almost none of the Mainstream children ever had. Both groups of children had moved, on average, three times since their birth. Both groups of families predominantly lived in single-family homes, although this was more true of the Mainstream families. Thirty percent of the Abecedarian families lived in apartments, most of which were subsidized low-income housing. The other kinds of residences were rare for both groups. The size of the Mainstream homes was larger, containing an average of eight rooms, but the Abecedarian homes were not small, containing an average of six rooms.

Plate 2.1 Houses were mostly single-family dwellings with sloping porches that provided the hub for social interaction among adults and children. (Photo by Jock Lauterer)

If you were to walk down the streets of Milltown in the late 1970s and early 1980s, you would see people of all ages sitting and talking on their front porches while the children played in the yards and streets. Most of the single-family dwellings were situated on older paved roads, which were often in need of repair. Some of the roads were unpaved, and were made up of the solid red clay dirt common among country roads in central North Carolina. The houses were generally grouped close to each other with just enough land separating the houses from the street for small children to play outdoor games with their friends. Like many yards in North Carolina, grass in front and in back of these homes was sparse and children played in the red clay earth or in the pine needles that covered much of the ground. Vestiges of traditional rural and farm living were revealed by the numerous vegetable gardens beside or in back of the houses.

The homes were mostly one-story, although occasionally

Plate 2.2 Houses were older but neat and clean. Children were well-dressed and play equipment, such as bicycles, seemed readily available. (Photo by Jock Lauterer)

Plate 2.3 Even when porches were not a part of the houses, adults were seen sitting outside under a tree or in the dirt roads. In this way, they participated in the social life of the community while monitoring their children's activities outside. (Photo by Jock Lauterer)

there were one or two two-story homes scattered along the way. These homes were rather old wooden structures in need of paint and general repair. Every now and then a house would have some broken windows which were boarded up to keep out intruders. Almost all the homes had a front porch with a sloping covered roof which lent protection from the sun and the infrequent rainfalls. Adults and children of all ages could be seen sitting on the porches in the early afternoon and into the late evening. Even though these homes were often in need of paint and some structural repairs, they were clearly cared for by the families and welcoming to friends and family.

Much of the socializing in the community occurred outside the homes, not only because it was a less private place but also because the weather in North Carolina permitted easy outdoor living most of the year with clear blue skies much of the time. Since sidewalks were almost non-existent, older children played kickball and other games freely in the streets. Parents watched their children play from their own front porch or their neighbor's. Occasionally, playing in the streets could be tragic – especially on the busier streets. One of our children was killed by a car as she darted out into the street in the downtown area. It was the summer before she would have entered kindergarten.

In the late 1970s and early 1980s these Black neighborhoods were slowly being taken over by investors who were erecting fashionable apartment buildings and condominiums to serve the growing college and business community of the larger area. Thus, there were pockets of small Black neighborhoods, only a few streets wide and long, scattered all over the new Milltown, remnants of the once all-Black community. It was not uncommon to see an impressive and immaculate condominium through the pine trees on the next street while walking down one of the old streets.

The low-income housing projects in which our children lived were scattered all around the more affluent University Town. In all the times we visited the projects never once did we see a White family. Thus these projects were really all-Black communities placed in the midst of mostly affluent White housing. Some of the projects had only 20 or so apartment units while others had hundreds. The smaller low-income housing projects tended to be the older ones and were nestled within quite established White neighborhoods. This was reflected by the more traditional architecture of the smaller housing projects and the large number of trees. The smaller projects also tended to be populated by an older group of adults. One of our children lived in a project for older adults because he was living with his grandmother. Because of her poor eyesight the grandmother had chosen to live in one of the very small projects that she judged to be safe, and one that was downtown so her grandson would be within walking distance to many of the stores and shops. These smaller units often contained a series of nicely spaced one-story buildings with a pleasant park-like area surrounding them. These apartments were well maintained and residents took pride in the appearance of the area.

The newer and more populated housing projects had a variety of living arrangements, and there was often a waiting list for the larger units that could accommodate a large family. Some of these projects had townhouse units while others were more apartment-like in nature. These newer projects attracted a younger group of adults, and the growing drug and crime problems tended to center in two or three of these larger projects in the University Town. Again, these projects had large outside play areas that were populated by children of all ages during the summer months. Even when families lived on the second or third floor of a building, much of their time in the warm weather was spent sitting or standing outside talking to friends. The architecture of the larger projects was more modern and there were fewer trees to soften the imposing structures.

Lastly there were families who lived on outlying farms. These homes were generally similar to the ones in the town, except they were on more land. Some of these farm families saw mostly kin and were certainly more isolated from much of the activity in Milltown. Other farm families actually had some formal residence in town but, because grandparents or other kin owned the farm, they spent much of their time there and the children often spent holidays and summer vacations helping on the family farm. Many children who did spend large amounts of time in Milltown had some links to kin who owned land in outlying areas. Thus most of our children who lived in Milltown

Plate 2.4   The houses on small farms were similar to the homes in the town. They were usually family-owned homesteads that had been handed down for hundreds of years, from generation to generation. (Photo by Jock Lauterer)

or University Town had important links to the outlying farm areas that created a sense of pride and preservation of the rural form of life of the past.

There were, of course, exceptions to these arrangements. There were a few families who lived in terrible conditions, regardless of what kind of housing they were in. These families often did not have kin support and the grinding poverty and crime made life for them unmanageable. For instance, in the process of trying to visit one family we discovered they had moved to some land out of town but we were not sure exactly where it was. After scouting out the land for about an hour and asking several people, including one man operating a trac-tor on the land where the family lived, we were directed to a small shack on the edge of a field. It was hard for us to believe that anyone could live in such a condition; this family was living in a one-room shack with no bathroom or cooking facilities.

Fortunately for the family, and especially for the children, social services had also tracked them down and there was to be some help to relocate all of them.

There were also families who lived in very comfortable middle-class neighborhoods. One of our mothers married and went on to become a bank teller. She and her family lived in a lovely ranch house on the edge of town with a beautifully manicured yard. Two of the children in the experimental sample were adopted by two African American staff members of the Frank Porter Graham Center. These two children lived in advantaged circumstances from early childhood.

No matter what the living arrangements of the families were, almost all the apartments and homes demonstrated pride by the way in which the home was decorated and maintained. Even if there were few material goods in the home, it was clear that care had been taken in making the house as comfortable as possible. Many of the homes had pictures of famous Black Americans like Martin Luther King and most displayed some of the triumphs of their children, be it athletic or academic accomplishments. Almost all families had a few books that could be seen on a table or bookshelf in the main living section of the home. A Bible was often visibly prominent, even if the family professed little religious affiliation.

The Home Communities of the Mainstream Children

The children from the Mainstream community lived mostly in one of the many middle-income subdivisions that were located within a few minutes of University Town. Most of the sub-divisions were almost exclusively White although there were a few integrated sections that contained middle-income Black families. Although some of the homes had wood or vinyl siding, the newer ranch houses were often built of brick, partly because of its availability in this area of the South and also because brick was less of an attraction for the termites that ate away at the foundations of homes. The homes were generally spacious with large yards and play areas for the children.

Because sidewalks were rare anywhere, except in the downtown areas of the town, children generally played in their backyards or in parks. Unlike the Abecedarian families, very few of the Mainstream adults or children could be seen socializing outdoors as you walked down the street. Front lawns were often carefully manicured and because there were almost no sidewalks, children were relegated to the backyards where pine trees often prohibited the growth of grass. Unlike homes in the colder areas of the United States most of these houses either had no garage at all or they had a "carport," a structure attached to the house through the roofline but containing either no walls or only a back wall. The roof is supported by pillars on the four corners while the floor is usually cement. Thus, a carport keeps the sun and rain off the car. The carports were often used as favorite play areas for the children during rainy or inclement weather when there was no car using it. It was especially good for roller skating or other activities that required a smooth surface. Most homes did not have basements, so outdoor play for children was the norm, even during the colder months.

Mainstream homes did not generally have large front porches unless the home was an older one. Thus, families did not spend time sitting out front but were often seen on decks at the back of the houses where there was more privacy. Decks were uncovered porches that often spanned the entire length of the back of the home. They were usually slightly raised off the ground and made of treated but unpainted lumber. You could usually enter the deck from a glass door on the back of the home. Even the smaller two-bedroom homes almost always had a deck on the back. The decks were used for entertainment in the warm weather and children often played on them as part of the play area in the backyard. Parents usually monitored their children's play from a window or glass door inside the house.

Like many other middle-class neighborhoods, the streets were quiet and people valued their privacy. It was rare that visitors or relatives would just drop over without calling first and, as we will see later, the playmates of the children were often selected by the mother and formally invited after school to their home.

The Abecedarian Families in the Preschool Years

The families in the Abecedarian project were almost all of African American descent. All the families were indigenous to the North Carolina area and most had long histories of family in the Piedmont area of North Carolina. These were families who had not chosen to move North and who were proud of their history and especially of their ties to the land. They were unlike those African American families in the large cities of the USA, such as those depicted in *There are no children here* (Kotlowitz, 1991), who had experienced crime, violence, and isolation from community support. Unlike Black families residing in many Northern and some large Southern cities, the Abecedarian families had extensive kin networks, many of which were tied to land in the North Carolina area. The families were indeed poor by any financial standard but many were not poor with respect to family and community support. These families were reminiscent of the ones described in *All our kin* (Stack, 1974) and *Ways with words* (Heath, 1983), families who had many strengths in spite of their economic and educational status.

At the children's birth the traditional prognostic indicators of future success were clearly poor (see table 2.2). Most of the families were female-headed ones. Their income was far below the poverty level, and the education and IQ of the mother suggested a poor economic future for her children. The children in the study were, by design, the most at-risk children in the community.

The children lived in family settings that were quite different from those that characterized the Mainstream families. Although no data were collected on the Mainstream families while the children were in preschool, an initial depiction of the ecology of the Abecedarian homes at ages 1 and 3 (Ramey, McGinness, Cross, Collier, & Barrie-Blackley, 1982) indicated that, overall, about half the homes had five or more people living there. Almost every household included another preschool child while most also had a school-age child living there as well. Most of the children also lived in a multiple family or intergenerational

Table 2.2 Demographic Data for the Abecedarian Children

	Group	
	Daycare intervention (n = 64)	No daycare intervention (n = 57)
Female-headed family	82.81%	77.19%
Mean financial income in year of birth	$1,230	$1,080
Mother's last grade achieved at child's birth	10.27	10.00
Mean maternal IQ at birth	84.92	84.19

family setting. Children usually shared a bed or a bedroom with someone else in the home (see table 2.3).

Campbell (1991) classified the living arrangements that characterized the families when our children were born and at 8 years of age. What is most striking is the change in arrangements between these two points. As depicted in table 2.4, 61 percent of the children in our sample were born into homes that contained people living in a complex multigenerational arrangement. By the time the children were 8 years of age this kind of complex living arrangement occurred only 5 percent of the time. There had been a shift, for the children, from living in a multigenerational household to living with their mothers in her own home or in the care of grandparents, foster, or adoptive family. Although this type of arrangement was predominant for the school-age children, the striking structural change did not reflect the kind of informal contact that relatives had with each other which was apparent in our interview data. So even if the children were not formally living under the same roof with relatives of various generations, they had great contact with them over the early school years, as will be seen in the next section.

Table 2.3 Information on the Physical Ecology of High-Risk Children in the First and Third Years of Life

Characteristic	1st year (n = 56) %	3rd year (n = 40) %
Number in household		
≤ 5	55	48
5–7	45	37
≥ 8	13	5
% houses with 1 or more other preschool children	98	100
% houses with 1 or more elementary school children	52	47
% houses with 1 or more junior or senior high school students	44	27
Type of housing		
Single family	53	35
Multiple family	47	65
Dilapidated	18	15
Sleeping in room with child		
1 or more preschool children	7	26
1 or more older children	41	33
1 or more adults	73	77
Families with 1 or more members who smoke	80	82

(Adapted from Ramey et al., 1982)

The Haskins Family Interviews

Ron Haskins, with only a little help from some of the rest of us, interviewed all the Abecedarian, Mainstream, and Alamance families as their children entered kindergarten. The interviews were conducted in the home and the mother was usually

Table 2.4 Percentage of Different Household Types of Abecedarian Children by Group at Birth and Age 8

| | Child age | | | |
| | Birth | | 8 years | |
Household type	Intervention (n = 56[a]) %	Non-Intervention (n = 54) %	Intervention (n = 56) %	Non-Intervention (n = 54) %
Intact (2 biological parents in own home)	23.2	25.9	19.6	18.5
Step-family (1 biological parent and mate, in own home)		1.8	7.1	16.7
Single parent in own home	12.5	7.4	37.5	44.4
Complex (multigenerational home, immediate family members)	60.7	55.6	5.4	5.6
Grandparents care for child			7.1	7.4
Adoptive family or mother			7.1	1.8
Foster care			3.6	
Joint custody				
"Other" (friends, shelters, relatives)	3.6	9.3	1.8	
Data missing			10.7	5.6

[a] One Intervention family enters twice because an older and a younger sibling were enrolled. (Adapted from Campbell, 1991)

the primary respondent, although fathers were included if they were present during the interview. The interview itself focussed on some specific questions but, in general, many of the questions were open-ended and the answers were later coded into categories based on the kinds of answers that were given. For instance, instead of asking a parent to choose from a list of alternatives, the opinions and values of the parent were elicited with questions like, "What pleases you the most about Shekita?" or, "What would you like Shekita to do when she grows up?" The questions generally probed about the parents' feelings about their community living situation and the support systems in the community, child-rearing practices, and general aspirations for their children as their children entered public school at 5 years of age.

The Neighborhoods of the Abecedarian and Mainstream Families

During the interview family members were asked questions about what they liked most and least about their neighborhood and about the dangers in their neighborhood. The most striking aspect of the results was the similarity among the answers given by both the Abecedarian and the Mainstream families, which are summarized in table 2.5.

When families were asked about what they liked most about their neighborhood the answers fell into five different categories, including: nice neighbors; a convenient location for access to services such as stores and schools; privacy from other people in the area; numerous and pleasant playmates for their children; and the beauty of the physical surroundings. For both groups, having nice neighbors and privacy were the best aspects of their current living situations. These two aspects seemed perfectly compatible with the way most of us run our lives. We value privacy but when we want to socialize we like to have friends in the area that we approve of and can have fun with.

When families were asked what they liked least about their neighborhood their responses could be put into five categories as well. These included: no negative aspects; dangers such as busy streets and bodies of water; unsavory or unpleasant neighbors; an inconvenient location far from friends and stores;

Table 2.5 Neighborhood Characteristics

	Abecedarian (n = 91) %	Mainstream (n = 70) %
What do you like most about your neighborhood?		
neighbors	21.95	30.00
convenient location	12.20	12.86
privacy	47.56	24.29
playmates for children	2.44	10.00
physical surroundings	10.98	17.14
other	0.00	1.43
What do you like least about your neighborhood?		
nothing	20.00	17.14
hazards	17.65	14.29
people	27.06	12.86
inconvenient location	3.53	7.14
poor physical surroundings	27.06	27.14
Afraid of stealing (no)	68.18	81.43
Afraid of violence (no)	82.95	94.29
Danger for children in your neighborhood (yes)	65.56	76.81
Type of danger		
traffic	61.02	56.60
bodies of water	13.56	9.43
dogs	13.56	9.43
snakes	5.08	13.21
woods	1.69	5.66
construction	1.69	3.77
other	0.00	1.89
Type of trouble caused by cults in neighborhood		
vandalism/theft, fights	11.11	11.11
noisy/profane language; gossip/yelling	41.85	44.44
drinking	7.41	11.11
guns	0.00	11.11

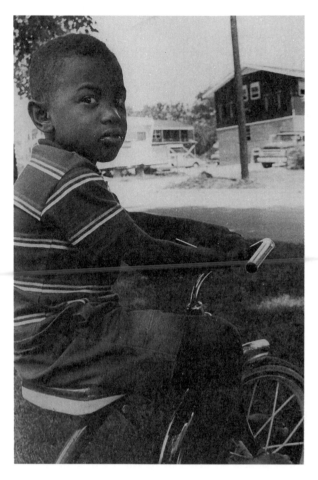

Plate 2.5 Without sidewalks, all children played in the family yard or in the street. Even in the heat of the summer and out of school, children took pride in their appearance and were clean and neatly dressed. (Photo by Jock Lauterer)

or unkempt physical surroundings. Again, the two groups of families were remarkably similar, although the Abecedarian families did report more dislike for the people living in their neighborhoods. This may have been due to the larger number of families in the Abecedarian sample living in housing projects where there was more noise and more problem families than in the single-family home neighborhoods.

When families were asked whether they worried about theft or violence in their neighborhood, most families, both Mainstream and Abecedarian, answered negatively. Thus, although the Abecedarian sample lived in poverty, they lived in relatively safe neighborhoods that were not described any differently from the neighborhoods of Mainstream families.

When asked specifically about whether there were dangers to children in the neighborhood, both groups reported that dangers did exist. In fact the Mainstream parents responded "yes" to this question more than the Abecedarian families. When asked what types of dangers existed for children, families again answered quite similarly. The danger of traffic and cars was clearly the major concern for both groups. This seems to be more a problem in the southern United States where there are no sidewalks except in the downtown areas and on major streets. Many children, even our Mainstream children, played in the street when they wanted to ride their bikes or play ball. There were only one or two families in the entire sample who had sidewalks outside their home. Thus, the danger of traffic was real, especially for young children who might not always follow traffic rules when playing in the street.

Bodies of water were mentioned as dangers because there were many ponds and creeks in the area that could be of danger to young children. Dogs were a danger almost everywhere since there are few leash laws in North Carolina. Even in the middle-class subdivisions dogs were allowed to run loose. Snakes have always posed a problem in the Piedmont area of North Carolina, since many poisonous snakes, like copperheads and water moccasins, are found frequently in people's backyards and in parks where children play most of the year. Because of these perceived dangers, all the children in both groups tended to play very close to home in a play area, the street, or the backyard, all within sight of a competent adult. Surprisingly, not one of the families reported danger due to other children or adults.

When asked what other kinds of trouble and danger were related to the adults living in the area, noisy, boisterous activity was rated by both groups of families as the most frequent cause of trouble, while theft and vandalism were listed by many families as much less of a problem. Thus the neighborhoods of both families were perceived as relatively safe but both groups agreed that there were dangers to children. These dangers appeared to be related more to the age of the child rather than to the kind of neighborhood. Again, the neighborhoods seemed to be rather benign, with families rarely talking about violent crime or drugs.

This feeling about the neighborhoods was certainly confirmed by our many excursions to the homes. There was only one time when I, as a researcher, felt unsafe. One day while I was observing one of the children, four tall muscular young men burst into the house unannounced and began talking excitedly to the mother in the house. My initial alarm at their sudden entry was unfounded as I realized these men were her cousins who had come to check up on her and to tease her for not having a large feast ready for them to eat.

Contacts with Extended Family in Abecedarian and Mainstream Families

Because of the diversity of family structure within the Abecedarian families, we asked a number of questions about family contact with friends and other extended family. Probably the most striking finding, although not the most surprising, was the role of kin in the lives of the Abecedarian children. Literally every family attended some kind of family reunion once a year. Distant relatives were reunited and family history was orally reconstructed. Haskins (Ramey & Haskins, 1981) reported that the children in the Abecedarian sample saw an average of 37 different relatives per month, 24 relatives from the mother's side of the family and 13 from the father's side. By contrast, the average middle-class Mainstream child in the same community saw an average of two relatives monthly, and the modal number was actually zero. This difference will later emerge when we describe the more detailed observations of the children's play in their neighborhoods during the afternoons after school. But this overwhelming difference must have played a major role in differentiating the family contexts of Mainstream versus Abecedarian children. Personally, it would be hard for me to even name 37 different people in my family, much less have them visit me each month.

When asked who would be called upon in a family emergency, 77 percent of the Abecedarian families reported that they would call upon a relative while only 36 percent of the Mainstream families said they would do so. On the other hand the Mainstream families reported that, in an emergency, 63 percent would call upon a friend or neighbor while only 16 percent of the Abecedarian sample reported this. This was even a more impressive difference since the Abecedarian families lived in more dense housing, having more opportunity to call on a neighbor than a middle-class Mainstream family. Clearly, the extended family was very important to the Abecedarian families and these kin probably had an impact on many aspects of the children's development.

Family Values, Aspirations, and Discipline Practices

There has been some debate about the role of family values, and of parental support and aspirations, in children's school functioning. Because the focus of this study was on the children's school functioning, it was important to understand how families viewed the role of the school as well as whether their aspirations for their child were synergistic with those of the school and the mainstream culture. Haskins was particularly interested in how the parents viewed certain child-rearing practices, especially with respect to whether these practices were similar to the ones used in the school context.

Families were also asked questions about their values, especially as they were related to their child. Most of the key questions and answers are summarized in table 2.6.

In general, over a third of the families in both groups reported attending church at least weekly. The Abecedarian families appeared to find church more important overall since 40 percent reported attending church at least once a month compared to 16 percent of the Mainstream families. Twice as many Mainstream families as Abecedarian were not regular churchgoers. This finding was coincident with the description of many African

American communities where the church has been seen as an important part of the life of the community (Poole, 1991; Hoots, 1993). This is especially true in the South where, until the second half of the twentieth century, the church has been bound up with schooling and the general child-rearing practices of the community.

Information about aspirations and the value of education with respect to the target child revealed few group differences. Again these answers are summarized in table 2.6. When asked about what they wanted their child to be like in high school, the Abecedarian parents were more likely than Mainstream parents to mention good academic skills and grades while the Mainstream parents were more likely to mention being well adjusted. Neither group rated being popular as an important aspiration. Thus all parents, but especially the Abecedarian families, saw academics as most important for their children. Parents were also asked about what they wanted their children to be when they grew up. Both groups of parents were very similar, both reporting that they either wanted their child to be whatever he/she wanted to be or they wanted their child to have a white collar or professional career. Asked if they wanted their children to go to college and had they saved money for college, both groups were remarkably similar, especially given their different economic circumstances. Almost all the parents wanted their children to go to college, and 40 percent of the Abecedarian group and 50 percent of the Mainstream group had saved money for their children's college education.

When parents were asked about what pleased them most about their child, the two most frequent answers were characteristics that represented loving and affectionate behavior as well as neat and organized behavior. Abecedarian parents placed more value on being neat and organized while Mainstream families valued loving and affectionate behavior. None of the families reported that the children's helpfulness around the house was what they liked best. As for the characteristics the parents liked least, they reported very similar kinds of annoyances common in 5-year-olds, including whiny and pouty behavior, teasing and verbally inappropriate behavior, as well as arguing and fighting.

In parental accounts of what kinds of child behaviors were

Table 2.6   Family Values, Aspirations, and Discipline

	Abecedarian (n = 91) %	Mainstream (n = 70) %
How often does family attend church?		
every week	37.50	38.24
at least once a month	40.00	16.18
once a year or less	22.45	45.59
What does your child do that pleases you most?		
helpful	6.67	5.80
loving/affectionate	30.00	62.32
clean/neat/organized	37.78	13.04
independent	6.67	5.80
nothing	1.11	0.00
everything	2.22	2.90
other	15.56	10.14
What bothers you the most about your child?		
whine/pout	20.88	20.29
argue/fight	14.29	14.49
not listen	3.30	11.59
tease/bad behavior	27.47	33.33
physical habit	12.09	7.26
nothing	8.79	5.80
other	13.19	7.25
What kind of punishable behavior does your child display?		
verbal annoyance	17.86	10.00
disobedient	29.76	20.00
destructive	5.95	8.57
fight/argue	20.24	34.29
negative personality	14.29	15.71
other	2.38	5.71

cont.

Table 2.6 (cont.)

	Abecedarian (n = 91) %	Mainstream (n = 70) %
What kind of punishment is used on your child?		
physical	47.66	26.08
withdraw privileges	20.34	4.35
time out	23.73	28.26
lecture or talk	6.78	39.13
make reparation	1.69	2.17
What do you want your child to be most like in high school?		
academic/good grades	47.25	28.99
well adjusted	20.88	44.93
athletic	14.29	5.80
social (popular)	7.69	11.59
don't know	5.49	0.00
other	4.40	8.70
What do you want your child to be when they grow up?		
professional	19.77	23.53
white collar job	15.12	0.00
whatever wants to be	39.53	45.59
don't know	5.81	14.71
other	19.77	16.18
Do you want your child to go to college?		
yes	89.53	88.24
no	0.00	0.00
if wants to	10.47	11.76
Have you saved money for college? (yes)	39.74	50.00

punishable, both sets of families answered similarly. Punishable behaviors included verbal annoyances, disobedience, fighting and arguing, having a negative attitude, and being destructive. The two groups of parents were not similar, though, in the kind of punishment they felt was appropriate. When asked about discipline procedures for punishable behaviors, it was clear from Haskins' interview as well as interviews with key people in the community, that discipline was viewed differently in the Abecedarian and the Mainstream groups.

In the Abecedarian families discipline was seen as not only the province of the nuclear family – many respected adults in the community had not only the right, but the duty, to discipline the children. Physical punishment was preferred and used by all responsible adults. The families recognized that the responsibility for child-rearing was shared among the elders in the community of people. (This communal view of discipline was also commented upon by Ward (1971) in her observations of Louisiana Cajun families.) This meant that the children understood that transgressions seen outside the home would not be tolerated. In addition, physical punishment was the norm and other relatives and respected adults were obliged to physically punish children for transgressions, even if they were not their own children. As can be seen in table 2.6, physical punishment was the most frequent kind of punishment for the Abecedarian parents while lecturing or talking it over was the most frequent punishment for the Mainstream parents.

Parents' comments about physical punishment indicated that they felt too many children in the Mainstream group and in school needed stricter discipline. They believed that this physical discipline would help their children develop a strong moral character that could help them cope with the world of discrimination in the larger community. They recognized that physical punishment was not accepted by the Mainstream community and especially the school. One mother told us that after she had recently spanked her 5-year-old daughter for disobedience, the child threatened to tell the social worker that she was being abused. The mother was somewhat surprised that such a young child could already play one adult's value against another's for her own benefit. The mother told us that this conflict between her strong-held views about the value of physical punishment and the more mainstream view had caused many of her friends and family difficulty with the social service system and the schools.

Overall then, the interview showed differences only on discipline between the two groups with the Abecedarian families using more physical punishment for transgressions. Both groups of families had aspirations for their children that indicated the importance of academic success in school.

Although only 17 Alamance county families were interviewed, this low-income White population was different from both the Abecedarian and Mainstream families in some quite specific ways. For instance, the Alamance families never described transgressions by their children as including verbal annoyances like talking back or interrupting the talk of others. They were more likely to want their children to be well liked rather than to do well academically in high school, and only about 50 percent of the parents had aspirations for their children to go to college. They also reported that the trouble caused by adults in the neighborhood was most frequently due to drinking, while drinking was infrequently mentioned by either of the other two groups.

Overall, the interview revealed few differences among the families with respect to their living conditions or values and aspirations for their children. The only major difference between the Abecedarian and Mainstream groups of families was the Abecedarian families' use of physical punishment for discipline; the Alamance families were a bit more dissimilar from both the other groups in their aspirations for their children and in their views on their neighborhood setting.

The Role of the Absent Father

Haskins was also interested in examining the role of the father, especially in the Abecedarian sample where nearly half the mothers had never married even as their children were entering school. All of the Mainstream mothers had married. Haskins has reported some information about the role of the father in these families (Haskins, 1988; Ramey & Haskins, 1981). Like many families on welfare, the father was usually absent from the family, but in our Abecedarian families this did not mean that the father did not contribute to the material well-being of the family or have frequent contact with them. In fact, evidence has been presented from the interviews with the Abecedarian families (Ramey & Haskins, 1981) that the father and the father's kin contributed money, food, clothing, and childcare in most of the cases where the father and mother were not living together.

This kind of informal support by the absent father has been difficult to measure in most studies, but Haskins (1988) tried to identify the sources of support in a large group of AFDC fathers compared to non-AFDC fathers in North Carolina. Aid to Families with Dependent Children (AFDC) is a federally funded welfare program for poor, single-parent (usually mother) families with dependent children. A prevalent American myth has been that these absent fathers do not contribute much to their children's well-being. Many of the families in our study were recipients of AFDC payments in the early years, and at the child's school entry one third of the mothers were continuing to receive AFDC. Thus the Haskins North Carolina study was representative of many of the families in the Abecedarian project. He found that AFDC fathers provided more non-court ordered support for their children; and that 65 percent of these AFDC fathers reported seeing their children at least once a week after separation and 59 percent were still maintaining visitation at least once a week. The non-AFDC fathers were basically more financially able, but had much less visitation; 32 percent saw their children at least weekly after separation and 40 percent reported seeing their children weekly at the time of the interview. The kind of contact with the father and his side of the family surely signaled to the child his commitment to their well-being.

The Schools

The children in this study were the first and second generation of children attending integrated schools. Milltown and the University Town shared a common school system. Schools were racially balanced, containing approximately 25 to 30 percent minority students who were almost exclusively African American. Like many other Southern school systems, race and socioeconomic status (SES) were confounded so that not only were Blacks at a disadvantage ethnically but also at a grave disadvantage economically compared to the White population. Some of the more rural schools that our children attended were even less ethnically diverse, with only a few minority pupils in each classroom. A fairly large industrial city nearby had not yet integrated with the suburban population; thus, the few children who attended school in that city had literally no White classmates and unbelievably substandard facilities. A small minority of our children attended these other types of schools; the vast majority (over 85 percent) attended a school within the school district containing Milltown and University Town.

The schools were not large, containing an average of about 300 children. Because of the lack of sidewalks and the redistricting due to integration in the primary school system, almost all children were bussed to school. Although the majority of teachers and school administrators were White, about 15 to 20 percent of the teachers were Black. Full-day schooling in North Carolina began immediately in kindergarten. All 5-year-old children had a long day, beginning at about 7:30 a.m. with a bus ride to the school and returning home between 2:30 and 3:00 p.m.

The philosophy of kindergarten changed somewhat over the years our children attended kindergarten, although there were always large individual differences among the teachers in the way they structured their program. When the first of our children entered kindergarten most of the classrooms were "open." School began with free play and then the children settled down to "circle time" where they all sat in a circle with the teacher. The day's schedule was laid out for them at that time and some large group activity, like "sharing," was conducted. The schedule generally consisted of small group instruction, i.e., ability group instruction and center time. The classrooms were set up to have centers that consisted of activities that the children could perform without much adult supervision.

As the years progressed kindergarten changed to a more academic focus. With a new governor of North Carolina in the late 1970s, changes occurred in education. The governor had mandated a reading aide in every classroom from kindergarten through sixth grade. Almost immediately the lower grades had this extra adult in the classroom and there was pressure to have even young children learn the basics of reading in kindergarten. Thus the changes that occurred for the children in our sample were both good and bad. The ratio of teacher to child changed quickly from 1:26 to 1:13 with the addition of the reading aide. This added help allowed one teacher to do individual or small group activities while the other monitored the rest of the class. On the other hand, the structure of the classrooms changed somewhat so that the academic demands on the children were greater. Even for the middle-class children these new demands were difficult, but most of them had the kinds of experiences in the home and parental involvement with the school needed to adapt successfully. Our children had a bit more trouble with this more structured atmosphere with its new demands, including endless worksheets.

We also observed children in the first and second grades. These classrooms were definitely more structured than kindergarten with children sitting at desks in rows or grouping the desks together to form a set of tables around the room. First and second grade were very focussed on the teaching of reading and it seemed that almost all of the large and small group activities emphasized letters and letter/sound correspondence. Children in these later grades left the main classroom for their weekly visits to the school library and art room. All schools had adequate playgrounds. Planned periods of play outside on these playgrounds, usually two 15-minute periods per day, was generally considered the favorite activity of the children. A more specific look at the activities in the classroom is described in more detail in chapter 5.

Most of the schools began before- and after-school programs by the late 1970s, but most of our Abecedarian children did not attend these programs since it was an additional cost for the families. Mainstream families used these programs more often, especially as the children entered first and second grade.

The Black Community, Church, and the School

The Black community considered this forced integration by redistricting to have both benefits and drawbacks. In the first half of the century in this area of North Carolina the Blacks worked in the White community but they lived in the Black community. Churches, schools, and even recreation activities, were completely segregated. Thus, the Black community had little control over the larger forces in the powerful White community and even in their workplace, but they had almost complete control over the community of people with whom they lived, including the schooling of their children.

The Black schools in the segregated areas before the 1960s were often situated on the same property as the church. This allowed a certain amount of access by both the church and the families. Recollections from those days indicated that children's schooling was the collective responsibility of the church, the family, and the school. Parents were often called into the school if their child misbehaved but it was also the responsibility of teachers and clergy to make sure that children were progressing through school. This kind of collective arrangement was severely disrupted by the introduction of integration.

Integration meant more and better access to resources that were not available in the Black schools but it also meant that the church and families were not nearly as involved in the school as they had been before. Discipline of children, which could be the province and duty of any respected elder, was severely disrupted, making many Black leaders feel that their children's access to public pools and movie theaters in the White areas meant that the Black community no longer had control over the activities of their youth. In the days of segregation, the church offered children the recreational activities that provided them with role models and the kind of learning that revolved around being a good and Christian person.

Today, the churches in Milltown have much less influence over young children and the community has seen some of their children lost to crime and drugs. They attribute many of these negative consequences to their lack of control over the children's lives in school and within the larger White community. Our informants reported that the youth often left the church completely, only to return later in adulthood after years of struggling for some adaptation to life in an integrated world. The churches are now trying to restructure some of their activities to address the radical changes that have occurred since the early 1970s. Some are instituting more attractive youth activities, but they have not been as successful as they would like to be.

Despite the changes that have occurred in the educational system, the church is still central to the lives of the Black family in North Carolina. In talking with families and informants, it is clear that the church continues to be the moral standard and produces the leadership of the Black community in Milltown. As Poole (1991) concluded in his review of the Black church in America,

> . . . the Black church continues to be the single most important organization in African-American life. Its prominence as the ethical center of the community stems from its status as the oldest social institution in African-American history. It remains as C. Eric Lincoln once declared "The spiritual fare of the Black community." This is so because the church continues to be one of the few organizations that is owned and governed by and is accountable to African Americans. (p. 43)

This was all the more important in Milltown where the Black community had a real sense of the history of their people in North Carolina, and where the church had stood by them and their families for many generations.

The parents of the children in the Abecedarian project were the first generation of integration while some had gone to segregated schools for at least part of their education. Thus, they often felt quite alienated from the integrated school setting. Even given this feeling of alienation, parents and other adults talked about their children's schools as good places. When asked how pleased they were with their child's teachers, all parents gave teachers very high ratings. Yet they often voiced concern about the materialism in the school and their lack of understanding and knowledge about what went on in school. For instance, one woman did not like the fact that her child seemed continually to want whatever the other children in his class had, material goods she could not provide for him. Families often felt intimidated by the parent–teacher conferences because of their formality and because the onus seemed to be on the parent to make sure their child behaved, so unlike the Black schools where the responsibility was shared by the community as a whole. For many families, school was the place that could help their children out of poverty and it was frustrating to them that the schools often did not seem to be able to help their children do well.

In summary, all the communities contained concerned families with remarkably similar goals and aspirations for their children. Even with the large economic-educational gap between the families, the communities within which the children lived were, for the most part, supportive of schooling and supportive of the kinds of values that Americans believe should guarantee at least a modicum of success in school.

Our intervention project was instituted to try to ensure school success by providing some of the educational resources that might not have been available to the Abecedarian families living in poverty. Certainly in the beginning we were quite naive about the other kinds of non-material resources these children would need to be successful in school, and even more naive about how difficult it would be to make changes in teachers and schools to ensure the success of our children.

Summary

This chapter described the communities and homes of the Abecedarian and Mainstream families. Interviews with parents about their children's transition to school revealed family values and attitudes about their children's future and the public schools that the children were entering. These data were obtained when the children were 5 years old and beginning kindergarten.

Despite the enormous economic gap between the Abecedarian families and the Mainstream families and the fact that most of the Abecedarian children were in one-parent families, the similarities among the families were quite remarkable. Both sets of families liked the neighborhoods in which they lived. They felt safe and generally liked their neighbors. Over half the families in both groups lived in a single-family dwelling, although more Mainstream families than Abecedarian families did so. When asked about their aspirations for their children and their values about education, both sets of families were very similar. They all valued school highly and wanted their children to do well.

There were only two areas of real difference between the two sets of families. The first was the contact that the children had with relatives. The Abecedarian children saw an average of 37 different relatives per month while the Mainstream families saw only two. This was really a reflection of the importance of the extended family in the Abecedarian families and their indigenous roots in the Piedmont area of North Carolina. The second major difference between the Abecedarian and Mainstream families was in the type of discipline used for child transgressions. Mainstream families were far less likely to use physical punishment with their children and less likely to allow other adults to discipline their children. Almost all the Abecedarian families used physical punishment and saw this as an important part of building morality and strength in their children. They also empowered other respected adults to discipline their children when needed.

The schools were integrated in Milltown and University Town so that approximately 25 percent of the children were African American and the rest were Caucasian in each of the six elementary schools. The schools were medium sized, each with about 300 students. In kindergarten most of the children were in open attractive classrooms. The teachers were mostly Caucasian with about 15–20 percent African American.

The description of the families, communities, and schools was a portrait of a semirural community in the Southern United States in which the transition to integrated schools was being made. Because of the confound between ethnicity and poverty in the United States and elsewhere around the world, this community was not atypical of many places that are trying to address the inequities created by historical prejudices.

3

The Carolina Abecedarian
Intervention Project

How can we save our children? How can we build a decent future for them? As a practical matter we need to think in terms of a continuum for education, from prenatal care through adult life. No single program is a panacea. We need many to span the main years of growth and development during early childhood – from enriched prenatal care, preventive pediatric care in infancy, and high quality day care, to parent education, social supports, and preschool education.

Hamburg, 1992, p. 149

The Carolina Abecedarian Project was begun in 1972 at the Frank Porter Graham Child Development Center at the University of North Carolina at Chapel Hill. This early education intervention project was innovative for its time and one of the very few programs in the country that could claim random assignment of children to an intervention and non-intervention group. There were high hopes that this kind of intervention could truly make a difference to the lives of children living in poverty. The families were recruited through social service agencies and public health clinics, generally through the local hospital. Families who were thought to be eligible, based on a general screening, were visited in their home by one of the project staff to explain the purpose of the study and to ascertain whether the family would be willing to participate. If families were interested the mother was asked to visit the Frank Porter Graham Child Development Center.

At the time of the woman's visit to the Center an interview was conducted to obtain detailed demographic information and to assess the mother's IQ. This information was then combined to form a High Risk Index. This index was developed as a "best guess" of the relative weights of various background and family factors that would put her child at risk for poor educational outcomes (Ramey & Smith, 1977; Ramey & Campbell, 1984). This risk index included such factors as mother's education, IQ, and family income (see table 3.1). Because of the confound between ethnicity and poverty, almost all the families who were eligible were African American. Although a family had to have a score of at least 11 on the High Risk Index to qualify for the study, the mean for the group as a whole was much higher ($M = 20.08$, $SD = 5.72$). Women were identified and accepted into the study while they were pregnant with the child we would follow. Only a few women had to be dropped from the study after the birth of their baby. This happened when a child was born with some biological or mental disability. We were only interested in children who were at risk for environmental reasons. Women had to agree to accept either group assignment (intervention or non-intervention) before the birth of their child.

Since children in each cohort were born within a short period of time of each other, qualified families were pair-matched whenever possible on sex of the child, maternal IQ, number of siblings, and High Risk Index scores. From each pair of children, one was randomly assigned to the intervention and one to the non-intervention group. Ramey et al. (1982) reported that of the 122 families who were eligible according to the High Risk Index, 121 agreed to participate, although only 111 agreed to their group assignment. In the preschool years three children died and one child was diagnosed as having biological retardation. By school age attrition due to a variety of other reasons reduced the number to approximately 96 children (Ramey & Campbell, 1991). No systematic effects due to attrition have been found (Martin, Ramey, & Ramey, 1990).

At school age the experimental intervention and the non-

Table 3.1 High Risk Index[a]

Factor	Weight
Mother's educational level (last grade completed)	
6	8
7	7
8	6
9	3
10	2
11	1
12	0
Father's educational level (last grade completed)	
6	8
7	7
8	6
9	3
10	2
11	1
12	0
Family income (per year) ($)	
1,000	8
1,001–2,000	7
2,001–3,000	6
3,001–4,000	5
4,001–5,000	4
5,001–6,000	0
Father absent for reasons other than health or death	3
Absence of maternal relatives in local area (i.e., parents, grandparents, or brothers or sisters of majority age)	3
Siblings of school age who are one or more grades behind age-appropriate grade or who score equivalently low on school-administered achievement tests	3
Payments received from welfare agencies within past 3 years	3

cont.

Table 3.1 (cont.)

Factor	Weight
Record of father's work indicates unstable and unskilled or semiskilled labor	3
Record of mother's or father's IQ indicates scores of 90 or below	3
Record of sibling's IQ indicates scores of 90 or below	3
Relevant social agencies in the community indicate that the family is in need of assistance	3
One or more members of the family has sought counseling or professional help in the past 3 years	1
Special circumstances not included in any of the above that are likely contributors to cultural or social disadvantage	1

[a] Criterion for inclusion in high-risk sample was a score of more than 11.

intervention control group were split again, producing four groups. Half of each original preschool group was randomly assigned to a school-age intervention group for the first three years in school. Thus there were four treatment groups: a group that received preschool and school-age intervention; a group that received only preschool intervention but no school-age intervention; a group that received no preschool intervention but received school-age intervention; and a final group that received no intervention either in preschool or at school age (see figure 3.1).

Although both the preschool and the school-age intervention were important aspects of the entire study, there were no effects of the school-age intervention on the language variables described here. Thus this intervention will be only briefly described.

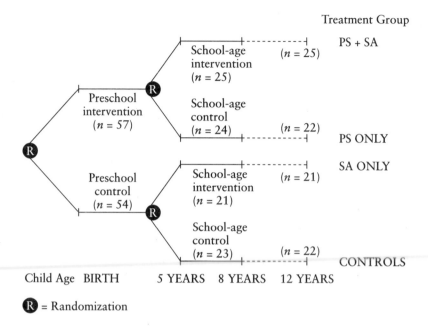

Figure 3.1 Study Design of the Carolina Abecedarian Project

The school-age intervention is described in more detail elsewhere (Ramey & Campbell, 1991; Campbell & Ramey, 1994), where they reported that the combination of the preschool and school-age interventions did have an effect on some academic indicators, but the more powerful intervention, even for these variables, was the children's preschool experience.

The school-age intervention itself was much less intense and relied on a home–school coordinator. This coordinator met several times a month with teachers and parents. The focus of the program was to give to parents, or other significant adults in the family, activities that were related to the work going on in the school. The home–school coordinator visited the classrooms and talked with the teachers to help develop appropriate and interesting projects to engage the interest of the adult and child at home. It certainly seemed to be a valuable addition to the intervention program yet it seemed to have little impact on the processes that will be discussed in this book.

The Daycare Intervention Program
(Birth to Five Years of Age)

As families qualified for the Abecedarian project the only primary difference between the infants in the daycare intervention and the non-intervention infants was the daycare program itself. In order to control for some of the variables that might confound the design, children in both groups received free nutritional supplements, including free iron-fortified Similac for the first 15 months of life. Pediatric care was obtained for all families through the Abecedarian project and through local pediatric clinics. Social services were made available on a priority basis for all families when it was deemed necessary.

Infants in the daycare intervention group began attending the center in the first few months of life (mean age at entry was 8.8 weeks) and they attended five days a week, 50 weeks a year until kindergarten entry. The program began at 7:30 a.m. and ended at 5:15 p.m. each day. In order to ensure full participation by all children a van was available each day to pick up the children from their homes and to return them in the evening.

The Physical Environment for the Intervention

All the children who participated in the intervention received the program at a University-run research center. A description of the physical environment can be found in detail elsewhere (Ramey et al., 1982; Ramey & Haskins, 1981; Ramey & Campbell, 1979). This center was located away from the university campus on property that also contained an elementary school where some of the Abecedarian children eventually attended public school. The research center was a four-story building adjacent to the elementary school and the children were cared for on three of the four floors.

Infants were cared for on a different floor from the other children. The nursery contained between 10 and 14 infants. Sleeping rooms were separate from activity areas. On a typical day teachers could be seen playing on the floor with two or, at the most, three infants. Schedules were flexible and children received much care and attention. In observations made in the daycare rooms (Farran, Burchinal, East, & Ramey, 1978) it was found that children spent disproportionate amounts of time with one caregiver and vice versa. Thus, although the intention was not to have teachers or children choose to interact with a particular person, this seemed to occur spontaneously as teachers and infants formed attachments to each other.

Once children were walking well (usually between 13 and 15 months) they were moved to the preschool floor. This floor was a large open space that was subdivided into a number of different rooms. Over the years the size and the composition of the groups changed. For instance, when the program began the children were almost entirely Abecedarian children; as the program evolved more middle-income and White children became part of the preschool program. This was done to create a more representative mix of children. Near the end of the project, children with disabilities were also part of the daycare mix of children. The size of the groups also changed. At first they were quite large with several teachers managing the group. Ages were segregated for institutional purposes. Over the years, group size tended to decrease and mixed-age groups were introduced to foster less competitive and more nurturing behavior for all the children. Thus, although the quality of care was maintained the spatial configurations and the composition of the groups changed somewhat over time as was needed to maintain or increase quality of care.

In the summer or fall before public school entry, children were transferred to more traditional-looking classrooms where the organization was more like a kindergarten classroom. Tables and work stations were arranged so that more structured activities could be accomplished for at least part of the day. Worksheets and other more formal types of independent work were presented to the child in an effort to make sure such activities would seem familiar upon school entry. The activities in these classrooms focussed more on preacademic skills.

There was a public school kindergarten on the bottom floor of the building. This was eventually eliminated in the middle of the intervention part of the project. There was also a play-room on the ground floor that preschoolers used for indoor rough-and-tumble play. Outside at the back of the building was a large playground area with age-appropriate play equipment, including bicycles, scooters, and other equipment for outdoor activities.

Teachers

The teachers who were hired to deliver the intervention program varied in background. Many were drawn from the same African American communities as the children and did not have as much formal education as the other teachers. Yet all the teachers had extensive experience with children and all were hired to provide a warm and supportive environment for the children. The teacher–infant ratio was 1:3, while the ratio in the toddler area and preschool classrooms was 1:4. The director of the intervention constantly provided workshops for the teachers and they were equipped with a large array of materials and taught new skills to make them more effective teachers.

Curriculum Development

The goal of the intervention program was to prevent school failure for children living in poverty. As Ramey and Campbell (1991) saw it, the program's "goal for families was to have a warm and friendly, homelike atmosphere that families would find helpful and positive. For children the goal was to provide them with a safe and healthful environment staffed by sensitive and resourceful early childhood educators who would offer high-quality education and emotional support" (p. 195).

The actual curriculum itself in the first three years was generated from four sources (Ramey & Haskins, 1981). The first included a Piagetian approach to learning. This meant emphasis on both cognitive and language skills within the context of the child acting on the environment by interacting with both peers and adults. Second, and in conjunction with the first, emphasis was placed on the achievement of developmental milestones as suggested by Gesell and Amatruda (1947), including motor, language, and cognitive tasks. Third, emphasis was placed on trying to instill behaviors – both social and attitudinal – that would facilitate learning. These included attention to task behaviors and socially interactive behaviors. Last, interviews with parents helped establish priorities for their children, some of which were discussed in the previous chapter; they included hoping that their child would be prepared for public school, and that they would learn how to adapt to the larger environment of the community. It is important to remember that formal parent involvement was not part of the Abecedarian intervention. Thus the daycare intervention sought the support of parents but they were minimally involved in the development of the curriculum itself or in the everyday running of the program.

The Overall Curriculum

Sparling and Lewis (1979) developed over 300 curriculum activities based on the above four areas. This curriculum was specially designed for our project and the kinds of teachers and parents we hoped would use these activities. Eventually the curriculum was published as a book for parents and teachers.

Our teachers were asked to use these 300 items as examples of how to encourage development in particular areas. The book was divided into sections based on the age of the child. Curriculum items in the various areas of development were explained very carefully with instructive photographs to help teachers and parents easily understand how to encourage the child to engage in the kinds of activities that would promote the curriculum goal.

For instance, an item in the first six months was called "Talking for Him to See." The item was explained in detail on one page and with pictures and a few words on another page. Each item was described by both "how" and "why." This particular item for an infant explained the "how" this way: "Hold your baby close so he can see your face and lips. Talk happily to him. Then pause and listen for him to make baby sounds. If he does, repeat his sounds. Let your face and voice show him you like it when he makes sound . . . because these little sounds are the bits and pieces from which he will later make words" (p. 25). The "why" is explained this way: "To help the baby know that sounds and mouth movements go together, and to encourage him to watch your face as you talk. To allow him to experience the pleasure of back and forth vocalization" (p. 24).

In the second year of life the goals were to encourage language comprehension and expression, and in the third year the items encouraged specific skill development of placement words like "on," "in," and "under" and time words like "when," "before," and "after." In addition there were also language items that encouraged children to talk about their lives. In one item called "Telling Family Stories" children were encouraged to collect pictures that looked like the people in their family. The pictures were then used as stimuli for the children to tell stories about events that happened to them at home.

After three years of age a variety of more standardized curriculum packages were used, many of which had a language focus. These included the *Peabody early education kit* (Dunn, Chun, Crowell, Dunn, Avery, & Yachel, 1976); language and cognitive activities that promoted cognitively based language and other skills, *Bridges to reading* (Greenberg & Epstein, 1973); a language-based social program called *My friends and me* (Davis, 1977); and a decoding pre-reading skill program developed by Wallach and Wallach (1976).

The Importance of Language in the Curriculum

As the curriculum was developed more emphasis was placed on developing not only language skills but narrative and discourse skills that required the child to communicate complicated information effectively. Ramey and Campbell (1991) articulated this emphasis within the Abecedarian intervention:

> Because a number of theorists have hypothesized that deficits (Blank, 1982; Tough, 1976) or differences (Heath, 1983; Labov, 1970) in the early language environments of disadvantaged

children leave them unprepared for success in mainstream public schools, language development was especially emphasized in the preschool program. The focus was on pragmatic features of adult–child language in the context of natural conversations about daily life. Teachers received specific training so that their verbal exchanges with the children would be developmentally appropriate and would elicit prolonged conversations (McGinness & Ramey, 1981; Ramey, McGinness, Cross, Collier, & Barrie-Blackley, 1982). In addition, preliteracy curricula were used with older preschool children (Greenberg & Epstein, 1973; Wallach & Wallach, 1976). (p. 196)

The work of both Tough (1976; 1977; 1982) and Blank (Blank, 1982; Blank et al., 1978) was used as the framework in which to create curricula to encourage children to talk at length about topics which they had some interest in and to encourage the children to expand on their utterances and to talk about the future and the past. This language intervention effort was developed by Sandi Barrie-Blackley and Gail McGinness (Ramey et al., 1982; McGinness, 1982).

Specifically, the evolving language curriculum emphasized eight categories of language use, seven of which were taken from Tough (1976; 1977). *Self-Maintaining* language referred to language related to one's own physical and psychological needs, for example, "I'm hungry" or "That makes me mad." *Directing* referred to language that directed their own and other's behavior, e.g., "Don't hit me" or "Give me that truck." *Reporting* was language that described or labeled objects and events, e.g., "There's a green ball" or "I see three boys over there." *Logical Reasoning* referred to language that explained relationships among objects and people in the environment, e.g., "The blue ball is bigger than the red one" or "My Mom is the best Mom in the whole world." *Predicting* was language that indicated that the child anticipated a future event or solution to a problem, e.g., "I'm going to the circus tomorrow" or "If you push this button the top of the box will open." *Imagining* referred to storytelling skills or the language of make-believe, e.g., "Once upon a time there was a big hairy monster" or "Yesterday my Mom and I went to the store and I pretended I was the Daddy." *Projecting* was language that empathized with the feelings and experiences of others, e.g., "If I were Little Red Riding Hood, I'd be scared, too" or "He must have liked having a new bicycle." The eighth category was added by the Abecedarian curriculum to help children develop good social and interpersonal language. This category was called *Interpersonal* and referred to language that offered praise or approval as well as reassurance to others, e.g., "You are a nice friend" or "Thanks for sharing the truck."

Workshops were conducted to help teachers monitor their own language and to help them use language that reflected the most abstract uses of language as much as possible. Teachers were helped to share language experiences with children rather than directing them as they used the eight categories. Emphasis was placed on trying to elicit as much language as possible from the children, especially language that developed a topic.

In order to help teachers elicit this language from children they were taught to monitor what was called an "information sharing/eliciting" strategy versus a "directive" strategy. Anyone who has worked with toddlers can vouch for the often overwhelming impulse to direct almost everything some of the toddlers do, especially when there are 10 or 15 of them running around a preschool classroom. Active toddlers may only seem to understand commands and to have an attention span that appears almost incapable of a reasoned dialogue. So, teachers practiced monitoring their own talk to the children. Consultants gave them periodic feedback so that informative talk might reach a level of 75 percent of the total talk. As one who observed the teachers on several occasions, I noted the monumental effort it took to achieve a high level of informative/eliciting talk and the even greater patience needed to deal with children who were more interested in wrestling with each other than conversing with an adult.

Although some children needed more practice with talk than others, it was thought by all of the professionals that the language curriculum could be used in any good childcare program (Ramey et al., 1982; McGinness, 1982). Although teachers varied quite a bit in their effectiveness as communicators and elicitors of language, the program was clearly high quality and the children seemed to enjoy their days at the center.

A Major Myth in Our Intervention

There was no doubt that there was an unwarranted assumption made by many of the intervention developers and the research staff. The project assumed that these high-risk poor children were not receiving the kind of language input at home that was needed for optimal development. The "middle class" standard bearer was still thought to be "what was best" for all children. Ramey et al. (1982) put it this way:

> The focus of our effort to date has been to promote a particular kind and amount of verbal interaction between teacher and day care pupil. The kind of verbal interaction is largely modeled on what a middle-class mother establishes with her child; the amount is rather higher, perhaps like what a tutorial hour might afford. Because our day care effort is competing with many hours of experience in another type of linguistic environment in the home, we have assumed that it cannot be as casual and diluted as normal family interaction. To raise certain types of linguistic functioning in the child's response hierarchy, then, we are trying to provide a large number of practice opportunities. (pp. 162–3)

Although Tough (1982) and Blank (1982) made it clear in their writing that the language of low-income children at home was often quite adequate and elaborated, they recognized that some of the uses of language did not fit well in the school setting. They both put the onus on teachers to try to adjust their teaching styles and interaction patterns to fit better with the language use patterns of these "at risk" children in helping them make the transition to school, but they also stressed teaching the child "school-like language skills." The Abecedarian project used the work of Tough and of Blank to develop a sensitive approach to the development of language use but it was also tinged by the assumptions made by the original deficit notions of the 1960s (Bernstein, 1961; Hess & Shipman, 1965). This kind of assumption resulted in the Abecedarian program having a more remediation-type approach to language and especially a compensatory notion in the philosophy behind the curriculum. As McGinness (1982) described the curriculum for the Abecedarian children she said:

However, it appears that the disabilities common to children with serious delays and disorders are not necessarily the disabilities displayed by children who simply use some linguistic functions with more frequency and facility than others. The strategies for impacting on a child's ability to use middle-class functions versus exclusively lower-class ones would seem to be to provide contexts and experiences that elicit those functions and models who exhibit good use of them. (p. 233)

Thus, the Abecedarian language curriculum was an interesting and innovative one but it was predicated on the assumption that the children in the Abecedarian project were not receiving the kind of language input at home that would foster high-level language and reasoning abilities and that the Abecedarian language program could help by intense language interactions between caregiver and child. In all our enthusiasm to help these children we had failed to recognize our own biases brought with us from the larger society.

In May 1980 a conference was convened to discuss the initial language results and to help us think more clearly about how to prepare these children for the demands of school (Feagans & Farran, 1982). There was a clear message from the conference participants that we really knew little about the language of these children in their home communities and that interventions should stem from language gathered in the home community and in the public schools the children would attend.

There was real skepticism by several of the participants about whether the Abecedarian children truly had any language deficits at all. Researchers like John Ogbu, who was a conference participant, felt that the failure of many African American children in school had little to do with language, among other skills, and more to do with the "castelike" nature of their status in American society. According to Ogbu (1991), African American people were a *castelike minority*, a group that was incorporated into a society involuntarily and permanently. The group had limited access to the social goods of the society, including education and jobs. He concluded convincingly in this way:

Although the classroom is the "scene of the battle" . . . where the school failure is achieved, the causes of the war lie beyond that field and include the historical and structural forces we have considered . . . These important forces cannot be captured easily or in the classroom. Even if ghetto children come to school without discourse and narrative skills, there still remains the question of why they do not learn enough of these skills in school to perform like white children from similar socioeconomic backgrounds who may also come to school without the same skills. (p. 134)

We took the comments from this conference seriously and more carefully documented home and school language. In the next chapters we will not be able to address the impact of the larger societal forces that shaped the lives of the Abecedarian children except in a very limited way, but we can hopefully dispel many of the myths about the language, homes, and communities of these children. In addition we may be able to elucidate a little more clearly why and how our and other early intervention programs have failed to provide the best preparation for success in the public schools.

Summary

The Abecedarian Project was first designed as an early intervention project for children born into poverty. Because of the confound of poverty and ethnicity in North Carolina all children but one were African American. The children in the study were randomly assigned at birth to a daycare intervention or no intervention group. The intervention began as full-time daycare at 3 months of age until public school entry at age 5. At public school entry the groups were randomly split again and half of each group received a supplemental school-age intervention of much less intensity. None of the measures reported here were affected by the elementary public school intervention so it was only briefly described.

The daycare intervention was housed at the Frank Porter Graham Child Development Center. Vans transported the children from their homes to the center in the morning and returned them home in the afternoon. The curriculum was heavily language-based and delivered by a combination of professionals and women from the home communities of the Abecedarian children. There was no formal parent involvement or home visiting component to the intervention, but many of the professionals involved had strong ties to the Black community and to the families they served.

The children in the non-daycare intervention group did receive free infant formula and disposable diapers in infancy and later received free social work services and medical care. Almost all of these children were eventually in some form of non-parental care but it was often with relatives or friends and began somewhat later in the toddler period.

This early daycare intervention project was one of the last and best studies in the United States of the effects of an intensive early intervention for children born into poverty. The data not only examined the specific effects of the intervention but chronicled the lives of these children from birth onward.

4
Language Use Out of School

Pupils are individual human beings who have learnt language in the process of learning to live the life of their communities: the whole process has taken place in the context of the patterns of relationships, habits and values that make up that specifically human environment. If we are to make sense of the pupil's problems and needs when he comes to use the language he has learnt in the context of the school, then we must be very clear about the processes by which he has learnt it, and the human environment in which the learning has taken place.

Doughty, Thornton, & Doughty, 1977, p. 169

The original purpose of collecting language samples in a naturalistic context outside of school was to better understand how children used language in their home community. When we first began to collect the language data, we were interested in answering some basic questions about how language use in the neighborhood setting differed from the language use in school. As we became more involved in collecting the language data we realized that we were gaining some insight into how these children were thinking about the important parts of their lives and how they were learning about their community and the important activities of interest in their community.

This chapter will try to describe the language and activities

of the children by using Rogoff's (1990) notion of apprenticeship and guided participation as a framework within which to
interpret the interactions we will describe. Rogoff's perspective
is embedded in a sociocultural perspective of development that
emphasizes the active role of the participant in social interaction. In her view, "cognitive development occurs through children's active participation in socioculturally organized activities
in which children manage their own roles and those of their
social partners, and their partners help to structure situations
that provide children with access to observe and participate in
culturally valued skills and perspectives" (Rogoff, 1993, p. 23).
The concept of guided participation stresses the mutual roles
of the children and their social partners, embedded as they are
in socioculturally structured activities.

> The concept (guided participation) incorporates both guidance
> and participation, as children engage in the culturally valued
> activities of their community. Guidance may be tacit or expli-
> cit, face to face or distal. Participation may be peripheral or
> central; what is key is participation in meaning – not necessar-
> ily in shared action of the moment. (p. 23)

Although this perspective emphasizes the learning of culturally important activities, we will extend its use to the learning
of cultural belief systems that can become powerful influences
on children's thinking about themselves and others. We will be
interested in how the children think about important activities
like school and how they depict these activities in their daily
play with each other.

A fairly recent description of the neighborhoods and homes
of African American children in North Carolina (Heath, 1983)
contributed substantially to our understanding of how preschool children live and talk in their communities. It also gave
us some insight into how the home communities of these children differed from the mainstream culture. Although the focus of
her book was not a comparison of home versus school, Heath's
description of the mainstream schools and the intervention
partnership she engendered with the teachers portrayed the
real need to use a different sociocultural perspective when view-
ing the African American child in a mainstream school. This

chapter will explore, in a bit more detail than Heath, the kinds of conversations and activities that the children participated in as they were making the transition to school and will try to describe some of the similarities and differences between the Mainstream and Abecedarian children in their use of language. Their conversations with others revealed not only social and linguistic competence, but also the way they thought about their lives as they participated in culturally important activities.

The Context of Language Interaction

Traditionally, the most important "naturalistic interaction" for children's development has often been assumed by developmental psychologists to take place within the mother–child context as well as the family context (eating dinner, storybook reading; Ninio, 1989; Snow, Barnes, Chandler, Goodman, & Hemphill, 1991; Gleason & Perlman, 1984), whether that be in a laboratory setting or in the home. These contexts for interaction are clearly important for the mainstream middle-class family but as the child grows older they are not the only contexts of importance, and as the child enters school the importance of the peer and community become greater. The assumptions about what are the important contexts are based on middle-class or mainstream culture. Many Abecedarian families we visited did not eat meals together because of work schedules and other demands on their time. Children were often shared by an extended family network so that observation of the nuclear family unit would not have always been appropriate for understanding the interactions that were important for the children's development.

In our study, we wanted to gather language out of school in settings and interactions that seemed important to the children and occupied a fairly large part of their time. In our study, this context for both groups of children was the context of interactions and play after school in the neighborhood. As we mentioned before, kindergarten in North Carolina was a full-day kindergarten which, for all of our children, made a long school day for 5-year-olds. Most children in our study were home before 3:00 p.m. Although some children played inside the home, most played outdoors since the weather remained warm for most of the fall months and because the outdoors gave them more access to and privacy with their friends and siblings. Children were usually summoned by an adult for a meal somewhere between 5:00 p.m. and 7:00 p.m. On school nights most children went to bed between 8:00 and 9:00 p.m., although clearly there were some exceptions. Thus this neighborhood context represented the children's contact with parents, other adults, and children between the end of the school day and when they were called home for the evening meal. We collected data in this setting during the children's transition to school in the fall of their kindergarten year.

The neighborhood context varied considerably from child to child and there was certainly more variability within the two groups of children than across them. The settings always included some peers and a few adults but otherwise the environments varied considerably. We followed children through corn fields, backyards, and woods. Although 90 percent of the observations took place outdoors, a few children spent much of their time in their bedroom, on a porch, or in the living area of the house. Some of our children played mostly alone or with only one friend; others played in a group of 18 to 20 children, ranging in age from 1 to 18 years of age.

Language in the Neighborhood

In conjunction with the Haskins study of the social behavior in the neighborhood, observations after school were conducted in three 40-minute sessions. At least two observers were present at each visit, both Black and White, and who had known these children for some time. Thus, there was a minimum of formality and the children seemed to trust that these adults were friendly and as nonintrusive as possible. On the second visit to the neighborhood, the children were introduced to our tape recorder with the wireless microphone, but during this second session no real language samples were collected. We had carefully packaged our sturdy tape recorder and FM receiver for the microphone into an orange backpack that could be worn by the observer. The target child was asked to wear a wireless microphone that was sewn inside a vest. The children could choose to wear either a plain brown vest or a cowboy-like vest. The microphone could pick up language clearly as far as 100 yards away, although the observer, clad with the orange backpack, tried to stay closer so that good contextual notes could be taken. These notes were crucial in the interpretation of the later transcribed language interactions.

On the third visit to the neighborhood, the child was again introduced to the tape recorder and the vest, but this time language was gathered in four 10-minute blocks. These blocks were chosen because, in many cases, the observer needed time between segments to write careful notes about the context of the interactions. In addition, the observers often needed time to recover from climbing on play equipment and running through the woods trying to keep up with active 5-year-olds. The vest did initially call attention to the target child and almost all the children made some mention of the tape recordings during the sessions, including commenting on its use and asking a few questions about the machine, which revealed that the children were certainly thinking about why and how these sessions were being conducted. A few examples given below show some of the thoughts children expressed during the sessions.

Abecedarian Boy to us: Does this tape know when I'm thinking: When I stop does it stop?, I mean when I stop thinking.

Mainstream Girl to a friend: You know what's in this jacket? There's a microphone. And inside the microphone, there's another microphone and so they can hear me. Um, the ladies over there, they just want to see how my friends talk about me.

Talk about the tape recording constituted only about 5 percent of all language in the sessions. In general, the children quickly forgot about our presence and went about the business of play. At the end of the entire session, children were allowed to listen to themselves on tape and they were given a small gift for helping us with our sessions.

The Neighborhood

There were clearly economic differences in the settings between the Abecedarian and the Mainstream group, but the similarities really outweighed the differences. Most children had large areas in which to play, whether it was a playground or a backyard. All seemed to have access to basic play materials like balls, bicycles, dolls, and materials for pretend play. Thus in reading the transcripts there would be few clues as to the economic conditions of the children.

There were two critical differences between the Abecedarian group and the Mainstream group with respect to the number and kind of people the children had contact with in the neighborhood. First, there were about three more people talking to the target child during the 40-minute sessions in the Abecedarian group in comparison to the Mainstream sample. Mainstream children interacted with an average of 4.5 people during the 40-minute sessions while the Abecedarian children interacted with an average of 7 people. The other major difference was the age range of the people the children interacted with during the session. Mainstream children tended to interact with children who were within a few years of their own age, even if the other child was a sibling. Abecedarian children interacted with a wider age range of children. Thus, some of the Abecedarian children interacted with infants as well as with older adolescents in the neighborhood. Other than these two differences, and the obvious economic gulf that separated the material goods available to the children, the settings were remarkably similar.

Coding the Language in the Neighborhood

The Children.   The children whose transcripts were used for analysis were a subsample of the children we observed. We randomly selected 10 boys and 10 girls from the pool of Abecedarian children and 10 boys and 10 girls from the Mainstream group of children. Although we were interested in the possible differences between children in the Abecedarian sample who had had early daycare intervention (experimental) and

Plate 4.1 Children of all ages played together in the Abecedarian communities. Outside play was most common because of the warm weather most of the year. (Photo by Jock Lauterer)

those who had not (control), we did not expect to find differences between the two Abecedarian groups of children on their use of language in their neighborhoods. Subsequent analyses confirmed there were no differences so the results presented here will focus on similarities and differences between children's talk in the Mainstream neighborhoods in University Town and children's talk in Milltown and surrounding neighborhoods. As it turned out, three of the Mainstream children were considered to be "at risk" and similar to our Abecedarian children: They were dropped from the sample. Therefore the results of the quantitative analysis of neighborhood language were based on 20 Abecedarian children and 17 Mainstream children. Thus we were comparing two extreme groups, with respect to their projected adjustment to school and to their future success in society at large.

The coding system used was devised to capture the larger units of talk that represented more the dialogic exchange among the children. We were interested in analyzing what the children talked about and how long they could sustain a dialogue on a topic. Thus we developed a multi-tiered coding system that tried to capture a number of important features of the dialogues in which children engaged during their play in the neighborhood. Inter-rater reliability was established for all categories coded and can be found in detail elsewhere (Feagans & Haskins, 1986).

We divided all transcripts into *topic episodes*. The episode was defined by the talk of the target child. When the child began to engage in talk with or without a partner, the length of talk time devoted to this topic determined the episode. A change in topic or a 5-second pause signaled the beginning of a new episode. Occasionally there were intrusions into the episode by some non-contingent response from the target child or another. As long as the next turn was still on the same topic the episode continued, although the non-contingent turn was not included in the data for that episode. Intrusions were examined separately.

The episodes were divided into four different types. *Monologues* were talk undirected to another person or talk directed to the child him/herself. *Dialogues* were talk with another partner. *Initiation/no response* was an ambiguous category. This occurred when the child appeared to initiate a conversation with someone but that person did not respond verbally and the talk was then redirected elsewhere. This often happened in the midst of a baseball game or some other large group activity where many children were vying for talk time. The final category of interest was *songs/rhyming games*. These were examined separately because they were repetitive memorized routines that could not be easily categorized under normal conversation with others.

There were many levels of the episodes that were coded for language. In order to examine the grammatical complexity of the talk in an episode we chose the utterance as the unit to analyze. An utterance was any communicative verbal expression of meaning by the child. Thus we included incomplete sentences if they were communicative as well as many elliptical sentences that implied previous shared knowledge among speakers and listeners.

The first language measures tried to capture the grammatical/syntactic complexity of the children's utterances within an episode. We used *mean length of utterance (MLU)* as one measure. Even though the children were at an age in which the length of the utterance is somewhat less useful as a measure of grammatical complexity, it was a useful measure to describe the utterances produced by the two groups of children. We used MLU in words rather than morphemes in order to avoid any bias against the use of Black Dialect.

In addition to MLU we also examined the portion of talk that contained a subordinate clause and thus could be classified as a *complex utterance*. In our analysis we counted the proportion of complex utterances in each episode. This measure, in combination with MLU, gave us some indication of grammatical complexity the children were using in talk with one another.

We also examined the different kinds of utterances children used. We primarily examined three types. First, we were interested in how many *questions* children asked; second, we were interested in how many directives or *imperatives* they used; and third, we were interested in the number of *statements* or declarative utterances made.

The next level of analysis was a description of the content of the children's talk by semantically coding the kinds of topics in children's verbal episodes. These were also aimed at trying to code the complexity of the topics.

Because of the past literature about the lack of the abstract nature of some children's language use (Bernstein, 1961; Hess and Shipman, 1965), we coded the abstractness of the language used by categorizing the episode topics as either *concrete* or *abstract*. *Concrete* topics included language about objects and events in the real world; *abstract* topics contained less reference to objects and activities in the real world, for example discussing the fairness of the rules of a game, or the psychological characteristics they valued in a friend. Another related aspect of complexity was whether the children could talk about the future and the past versus the present. We coded whether the children's episodes contained reference to the here and now (*the present*) or whether the children reminisced about the past or made projections into the future (*non-present*), the latter being considered more abstract.

We also scored the sheer number of words children produced as well as the number of dialogues or episodes they were involved in over the 40-minute session. These levels of language analysis represented an overall picture of the children's language, using traditional measures of language ability.

We analyzed all of these language measures to describe differences by group and by sex. There were almost no group differences or interactions, and they were insignificant in comparison to the overwhelming similarity between the groups of children. This is especially important to note, given the disparity between the groups in economic and educational circumstances.

Structural Characteristics of Neighborhood Talk

An overview of the similarities between the groups will be presented first and then a discussion of some of the interesting differences will be offered. Although it may seem somewhat tedious to go through these similarities, it is important to do so because so much has been made of language differences between poor and mainstream children, especially when the poor children are African American.

Children talked with an average of 5.6 different people during the 40-minute segments; 1.8 of these people were adults. Children talked a lot during the sessions; they engaged in an average of 18 episodes over the 40 minutes. These episodes were characterized by having 6.5 exchanges on a topic and the target child spoke an average of 7.7 utterances. Thus most of the conversations were relatively short, with only one utterance per turn in a conversation, but there were clearly some dialogues that, once transcribed, continued for pages and pages of the transcript while others were only one turn long.

Children in the Abecedarian group had more people present during the 40-minute sessions in comparison to the children from the Mainstream group (7.0 versus 4.6). In addition, the Abecedarian children talked with children who were from a broader age range than did the Mainstream children. The Abecedarian children were observed playing with children from 1 to 18 years of age while the Mainstream children played with children ranging in age from 3 to 10 years. These differences reflected the context of extended family and community within the African American culture versus the more isolated nuclear family context of the Mainstream children.

Grammatical and Semantic Complexity: No Group or Sex Differences

When we examined the linguistic elements in each dialogue we found striking similarities between groups. All children used few *complex* sentences (5 percent) and in general their sentences were short, containing four words. About 14 percent of the time they used *imperatives* (directives) and 16 percent of the time they asked *questions*. The rest (70 percent) were *statements*. Thus, both groups used the same level of complexity and the same kinds of sentence structures.

As we just described, we were also interested in whether the children could talk about complex topics and whether the topic complexity would differentiate the groups. Thus we coded each dialogue or monologue for the level of abstractness, including whether the topic focussed on something *concrete* like a ball or on something *abstract* like the rules of a game and whether talk was about the *present* versus *non-present*. About 80 percent of the time the children talked about concrete objects in the environment and 90 percent of their talk was about the present. Again, there were no group differences.

Although *elliptical* utterances do not really index non-complexity in language use, it could be argued that it is a more familiar way of speaking, such that people who have shared information may use more elliptical utterances because only the new information needs to be explicitly stated. These are utterances that, in isolation, appear to be incomplete sentences but in the context of conversations are actually more appropriate. The following short dialogue includes some ellip-tical sentences.

> *Child 1:* Where are you going?
> *Child 2:* Home. *(elliptical)*
> *Child 1:* Why do you have to go home now when we are just beginning a good game of kickball?
> *Child 2:* Cause we have dinner now and Mom would be really mad. *(elliptical)*

Bernstein's (1961) notion of the restricted code might be reflected in the use of more elliptical utterances since in the use of this code information is not explicitly verbally stated. We examined whether the groups differed in the use of elliptical utterances. We found no group differences on these variables. Thus, there was no evidence from a quantitative analysis that either group had an advantage in terms of linguistic complexity or in the abstract level of their talk.

Total Talk

The only area of language where we found some differences was the amount of talk. The interaction between group and sex was significant in our analyses, indicating that Black boys used more utterances and more words per episode but engaged in fewer episodes overall than the other groups. When we looked at this interaction over the total session, the differences were very dramatic, with Black girls using the lowest number of words ($M = 487$) and Black boys using the most ($M = 698$). The number of words used by Mainstream girls ($M = 544$) and Mainstream boys ($M = 517$) did not significantly differ. These same kind of sex differences have been reported by Heath (1983) at even younger ages in African American children in North Carolina.

> . . . girls in Trackton begin participation in the third stage – that of entering conversations and adding new discourse topics – later than the boys. Boys sometimes begin to do this by about fourteen to sixteen months and consistently interrupt adults with these attempts by the age of eighteen months. No girls

begin the participatory stage before the age of twenty-two months, and when they do so, they are successful in sustaining conversational roles far less frequently than boys . . . When boys make these interruptions, they often refer to events or objects connected with challenges and ensuing interactions from the public stage. Girls, however, are restricted from engaging in such challenges since these are not issued to them. (pp. 95–6)

The Black girls' fewer words were probably due in part to their engagement in ritualized games and songs, discussed later in this chapter. Our qualitative analysis will clarify a bit more clearly why we may have found some differences, favoring the Abecedarian group, especially the boys.

Topics of Discussion in Children's Talk

Although our quantitative analyses were important to descriptively corroborate others' findings that the dialogues and monologues of all the children were relatively short and contained similar linguistic features, these analyses did not address the real content issue that might truly differentiate the groups. We were interested in a number of content areas and topic areas in order to better characterize the real experiences of the children in their communities. We were especially interested in capturing socioculturally important activities that would exemplify guided participation and apprenticeship in the neighborhood context. We chose a somewhat larger sample of transcripts in the qualitative analysis because we wanted to have as large a sample as possible to find recurring themes and activities. We chose to randomly select 15 Mainstream girls and 15 Mainstream boys as well as a like number of Abecedarian children.

In order to examine possible differences in the talk about important topics we tried to classify the most frequently recurring themes and activities in the conversations of our children, along with some a priori categories we were particularly interested in describing. In characterizing the transcripts we came up with four major thematic activities that dominated the dialogues and monologues of the children. These included *Sibling rivalry, Pretend play/Storytelling, Playing to win versus playing to play*, and *School talk*. The two a priori categories were school talk and pretend play and storytelling. These four themes captured over 60 percent of the conversations and monologues we collected. There were other activities, like riding big wheels and running through the woods. These activities did take up considerable time during the sessions but they did not contain very much talk because the gross motor activity generally dominated the whole activity. Thus our categories really captured the kinds of talk activities that children engaged in with other children and adults in their communities after school.

Sibling Rivalry

One dominant activity in many of the transcripts was the sophisticated interactions among siblings, both older and younger. Nearly 70 percent of the children interacted with a sibling during at least part of a session. Dunn and Kendrick (1982) described in detail how siblings affect each other's development from a very early age. Their descriptions of the interactions of siblings in the preschool period testify to the complex reasoning and sophisticated humor that can emerge from these positive and negative interactions (Dunn, 1985; Dunn, 1988; Dunn & Kendrick, 1982). Dunn argued that the sibling relationship is important in the child's emerging knowledge about social understanding and emotional empathy. It seemed clear that even in the preschool period children's emerging social understanding was clearly underestimated. The interactions presented here are also examples of the kind of apprenticeship that Rogoff (1990) described. As will be seen in some of the examples of these interactions, siblings were learning from one another some of the important culturally acceptable ways of interaction as well as learning content-relevant skills from each other. This seemed especially true in their interactions that included some rivalry or competition with each other.

In sibling conversations between slightly older children than those studied by Dunn, we found especially poignant examples of the complex relationships between siblings and, especially at 5 years of age, their ability to tease, educate, compete with, and enjoy each other all in one interaction without outright aggression or insults to the other. In both the Mainstream and Abecedarian children we found few differences in the way siblings teased and conspired against each other as well as in the shared intimacy between them. These children seemed to be learning how to win and lose successfully within the family and, at least in our presence, they showed surprising equanimity. We observed no instances of real cruelty toward or received from a sibling. There was a subtle sophistication in the interaction of siblings, such that they conveyed to each other the many conflicting messages that characterized their relationship. We saw many instances of the ability to free oneself from synchrony and reciprocity that reflected the children's ability to sustain a difficult interaction (Cairns, 1979). Although siblings occasionally fought with one another it was less common than the frequency with which it occurred with friends. We observed only six actual physical fights, two of which were between siblings and four were with friends. The following four conversations illustrate the kinds of complex conversational activities we observed.

The first interaction is among three siblings and a friend. Bernice is the target child from the Abecedarian group. The children are playing on a deck that is at least one story high at one end. The railing is such that the children can crawl under the railing and sit with their legs dangling over the edge. The three boys are doing just that and Bernice is standing back observing them. The two older boys are purposely enticing the 4-year-old (Bobby) to jump in an effort to irritate their sister, who knows it would be dangerous for any of them to jump, but especially her younger brother.

> *Bernice – 5 years (target child)*
> *Bobby – 4 years (younger brother)*
> *William – 8 years (older brother)*
> *Mike – 11 years (friend)*

William: Hey Mike you gonna jump?
Bernice: Bobby you better know, you better not jump down.
          I'm gonna tell Momma.
          (Bobby watches the two older boys leaning forward as if they are about to jump off the deck, but they don't)

Mike: Jump William.
Bernice: Bobby, I'm gonna tell Mommy you jumped down
            there. I'm gonna tell her you jumped down there.
Bobby: I'm gonna jump down.
William: No, you don't little guy.
            (William holds Bobby back from the edge)
Bernice: Mom . . . *(calls inside the house)*
Mother: What?
            (from inside the house)
Bernice: Bobby's gonna jump down off of the porch.
Mother: If you jump down I'll beat you if you do.
            (from inside the house)
Bernice: Bobby, Mommy says she's gonna beat you half to
            death.
            (Boys all laugh, Bernice frowns)

This interaction can be seen as superficially simple, but within
the interaction there is a display of teasing, competition, and
role-playing that represents the complexity of sibling relationships. Jointly they are partners learning from each other the
cultural activity of "mothering" as well as how this activity
can be thwarted by children. Many of the conversations were
like this one, with an older sibling trying to dominate a younger
sibling but the younger sibling almost never completely sub-
mitting while finding ways to avoid some or all of the demands
of the older child. The negotiation that takes place can be quite
impressive, leaving both feeling good about their role in the
conversation. In this case Bernice is being teased by the boys.
They really have no intention of jumping but they know they
can get Bernice to try her "mothering" role if they pretend.
Bernice falls for their ploy and tattles on Bobby because the
boys have led her to believe Bobby really will jump. In the end
Bernice loses, but the good-natured laughs of the boys make it
hard for her to stay upset.

The next conversation is a good example of the winning that
both older and younger children can achieve and the equanimity of both in the struggle. In this conversation, three girls are
outside playing in their yard. The home has a long driveway
with the mailbox at the end. The girls have been having races
around the house and down the driveway. Sasha, our target

Mainstream child, always loses while the two older girls alternate in winning. The two older girls are having a great time but Sasha gets frustrated at always losing as they decide to race to the mailbox once again.

Sasha – 5 years (target child)
Teresa – 10 years (older sister)
Marta – 6 years (friend)

Teresa:	I'll race again.
Marta:	Okay.
Sasha:	Not yet.
Marta:	Ya wanna race?
	Ya wanna race?
Sasha:	I get a head start.
Teresa:	Okay. Have a head start.
Sasha:	You gotta come by this way.
Teresa:	Straight to the mailbox. Sasha, straight to the mailbox.
Sasha:	No, stop. I get a head start.
Teresa:	I let you have a head start.
Sasha:	Let me have a head start up here.
Teresa:	Okay.
	(All run to mailbox – Sasha loses. Even though she has lost, she retrieves the mail from the mailbox before anyone else can.)
Sasha:	Here's the mail.

In the end the older sister recognizes that her younger sister needs to feel that she has won in some way. The response of grabbing the mail actually saves and sustains the interaction and the older sister appears to recognize it since she does not protest her younger sister's action. She smiles when Sasha retrieves the mail and they go on with the racing again for a while, with Sasha always getting a head start. This kind of activity is one in which all the children are learning together about the limits of competition and the way in which it may be fair to give a younger child a certain advantage. Learning to negotiate the relationship with a sibling, and the recognition by the older sister in the end that she needs to allow her younger sister to "win" the letters in the mailbox, is an example of the kind of appropriation that Rogoff (in press) talks about.

She views many of the social interactions among children as ways of changing the way the children view the activity and the successful participation in the activity. In the above example the older sister allowed her younger sister to "win" something because she realized that her sister's losing each race was about to end the game. According to Rogoff this appropriation occurs when children "puzzle out how to manage a new situation on the basis of their own and their shared history, to reach their own and their shared goals through emotional, nonverbal, and verbal communication indicating what kind of a situation this is" (p. 41).

Twenty minutes after this first interaction occurs the three girls are sitting on some rocks in the woods. They are picking up rocks, commenting about which ones are the best.

> *(In large and spacious backyard in woods sitting on rocks)*
>
> *Teresa:* This is my lucky rock.
> *Marta:* This is mine.
> *Sasha:* This is mine.
> *Marta:* This is my rock. It's a specialty rock.
> *Sasha:* This is mine.
> *(Older sister drops the rock on her own foot by mistake)*
> *Teresa:* Ooh, that hurts.
> *Sasha:* Does not.
> *Marta:* Hey, hey, hey
> *Sasha:* *(teasing sister)* Hey, hey, hey Fat Albert.
> *Teresa:* *(in anger)* Take a bite whenever you like. *(Referring to the rock)*
> *Sasha:* Hey, that hurts. *(Tries to take a bite)*

In this interaction, it is the youngest child who is learning how to be sensitive to her older sister. Sasha had called her sister "Fat Albert" and her sister, who was slightly overweight, was clearly offended. Teresa's anger was evident when she said "Take a bite whenever you like." Sasha indirectly indicates her apology by trying to take a bite out of the rock to punish herself. Her older sister recognizes the attempt of reconciliation and they go on throwing rocks in the stream nearby.

These two interactions illustrate the sensitive recognition by both girls of the needs of the other and they are learning how to negotiate their relationship as they cooperate in play with each other. As Dunn has observed in her sibling studies, the children can sometimes show great sophistication in taking the other's point of view. This ability to gauge the emotions of another and respond effectively, although not always graciously, can be seen much more clearly between siblings than between friends.

The last interaction example is one between an older boy and his younger sister. This contains some of the most sophisticated maneuvering by a younger sister that we observed, but it is a good example of how teasing and intimacy can be a large part of the sibling relationship. Both groups of children showed this kind of intimacy in relationships, especially with siblings. By intimacy we mean any secrets and confidences that are only shared between the two participants in the conversation. Confidences were shared twice as often between siblings in comparison to friends, even though the children interacted more with friends than with siblings. These confidences were often exploited by one of the siblings later but they still seemed to serve to bond the two together in a special way. This can be seen in this next conversation between Jon and Rachel. They are in the backyard of their house and Jon has a whip which he has snapped near his sister to annoy her.

Jon – 5 years (target child)
Rachel – 4 years (younger sister)

Rachel: Careful of my face.
Jon: I won't be careful of your face.
I'll be careful of your penis.
(both laugh)
Rachel: I don't have one.
Jon: I'll be careful of your pagina then.
Rachel: It's not called a pagina. And will you stop talking about those things.
Jon: Yeah, I'll stop talking about those things, if you'll stop talking to your friends about what color underwear I have on.
Rachel: I haven't been. Anyhow what color of underwear do you have? I won't tell any of my friends if you do tell me.

Jon: OK.
Rachel: Alright.
Jon: Blue.
Rachel: Jon you just said that on the microphone.
Jon: Oh no!
Rachel: I still won't tell anybody anything.

Although the two are clearly competing with each other to annoy each other, they are also confiding in one another. Rachel cannot, in the end, resist telling Jon that what he said was being taped, but his consternation was mitigated by her promise that at least she would not tell anybody else. Thus this 4-year-old won both ways. She certainly "got" her brother but she also seemed to understand the limits of her teasing and that some reparation would be needed if they were to go on playing. The sibling rivalry dialogues were the best examples of asynchronous responses: ones that, according to Cairns (1979), are not responses of the same kind or level but they can lessen the chance for confrontational exchanges. These young children had apparently already learned the subtle asynchronous ways to "get at" each other without making their sibling leave the interaction or play sequence completely.

Pretend Play and Storytelling

Children's play together regularly involves pretend and imaginary play. This kind of play is very conducive to the kind of apprenticeship that Rogoff has described where one child either models higher-level behavior in play or may be the leader or instigator of imaginative and creative play. This is the kind of play so highly valued in preschool programs, which is thought to enhance social and empathic skills and is also thought to be the precursor of the ability to create well-formed narratives and stories. Some have argued that these skills form the basis for the kinds of language skills needed in school (Blank et al., 1978; Feagans & Farran, 1982). Indeed, a large literature has now emerged on the precursors of literacy skills: These include joint bookreading and storytelling (Ninio, 1980; Wells, 1981; Snow et al., 1991).

Although we did not find any qualitative group differences in sibling competitive and teasing play, we did find quite striking group differences in the quality of the pretend play among peers and siblings. These differences favored the Abecedarian groups. We saw four times as many conversations in the Abecedarian groups which focussed on elaborated pretend play or storytelling. This was probably the case because African American culture supports what I like to call the construction of "joint storytelling." This incorporates some of the elements of guided participation in apprenticeship (Rogoff, 1990) among peers and reflects the cooperative venture that is culturally valued in the African American culture in such activities as creating imaginative stories. In joint storytelling, there is usually participation by at least one other person. This person may merely comment on the story as it is created or they may add to it to make it more elaborated. In any case, the joint participation makes this activity especially salient in the neighborhood where children and adults participate together in the development of elaborated verbal play and storytelling.

These differences can be seen in the following examples of cooperative pretend play in the two groups. The first two joint narratives involve the play of two African American children in each conversation. A high level of imagination and theme development can be seen in both of these. There were literally no examples of this level of storymaking in the Mainstream group. In the first joint play, Ricky and Dwayne are playing in the dirt by the side of Dwayne's house. The pipe they have found in the dirt initially looks like an old twisted drainpipe from inside a house but, as Ricky describes it, the pipe is transformed into a man in this richly dramatized talk.

 Dwayne – 5 years (target child)
 Ricky – 9 years

   (While Ricky and Dwayne are playing in the dirt
   beside Dwayne's house, Ricky finds an old metal
   pipe with twisted extensions protruding from the
   barrel of the pipe. This sparks his imagination as he
   begins to see the pipe as a man.)
 Ricky: Look at this man.

Plate 4.2 Pretend play and storytelling were central parts of the play of the Abecedarian children. This often occurred outside with many children participating. (Photo by Jock Lauterer)

    Dwayne: This ain't no man.
    Ricky: I know it.
                But look at this man with a light in his hand.
                It's a heavy man
                That's his, his head
                That's his hand and . . .

Dwayne:	Where?
Ricky:	That's his, his hand.
	He got a light in his hand.
	He got a light in his hand.
	He's a monster with a light in his hand.
Dwayne:	Oh.
Ricky:	He got no eyes. He can't see.
Dwayne:	Don't tell – that's enough
	(Ricky has begun slowly to modulate his voice rhyth-mically as he looks piercingly into Dwayne's eyes. Dwayne looks frightened and picks up a rock to throw at the Pipe Man.)
Mother:	Don't hit Ricky with that.
Dwayne:	I'm goin to beat that man up – right there.
Ricky:	Don't hit him.
	Don't hit him.
Dwayne:	Ooh. Ooh.
	What's in the middle there?
	(Points to dirt in front of pipe)
Ricky:	I'm goin to put it in there.
	That's broken glass.
Dwayne:	Stop bothering my glass.
Ricky:	We're goin to make a witches pool.
	(Ricky has made a hole in the ground and the broken glass serves as noodles)
Dwayne:	That glass.
Ricky:	I'm goin to make a witches pool.
Dwayne:	Why?
Ricky:	Put that noodles in it.
Dwayne:	That ain't no noodles.
Ricky:	I know it. It's all broken. Put noodles in it.
Dwayne:	The noodles?
Ricky:	We're making a witches pool.
Dwayne:	Oh.
Ricky:	We're making a witches pool. We two witches, making witches pool. We're putting lizards and snakes in it.
Dwayne:	Yeah!
Ricky:	One by one. Look at all those lizards and snakes. That's why we eat lizards and snakes cause we're the ones.
Mother:	Now you know better than that. Listen now. Richard. This is dangerous. You don't play with glass. You could cut yourself. Find somethin else to do.

The apprenticeship concept is certainly evident in this joint play. Ricky, as the older child, is helping Dwayne take some small steps in the culturally valued activity of image and story creation. Even though Dwayne resists the attempts of Ricky initially, Ricky persists until Dwayne really becomes a part of the rich images being created by Ricky's lyrical and almost haunting voice. The rhythmic quality of Ricky's speech builds as he progresses through building these images for Dwayne, who by the end is mesmerized by the entire endeavor, only to be brought back to reality by the reprimand of Dwayne's mother. This kind of guided participation certainly engaged the interest of the younger child and created the kind of involved environment that is needed for optimal participatory learning.

The other example from the Abecedarian children is Kenya, who is playing with her cousin and little sister in the tall grass behind their house. Kenya is on her hands and knees in the grass roaring and looking like quite a ferocious monster, tiger, and lion.

> *Kenya – 5 years (target child)*
> *Squirt – 6 years (cousin)*
> *Latif – 2 years (sister)*

Kenya:	Squirt, I'm a monster
	(Roars)
Squirt:	A monster!
Latif:	*(Laughs)*
Kenya:	*(Roars)*
	Hey Squirt, I'm getting something to drink. I want a drink.
	Squirt, pretend you don't know a monster is coming. You asleep and you don't know.
	It's coming! Whooo! Whooo!
	Pretend you asleep and you don't know. Pretend you asleep and you don't know.
	Whooo! He's comin, he comin.
Squirt:	You supposed to crawl Kenya.
Kenya:	OK.
Latif:	Whoa!
Squirt:	Crawl, crawl in the grass.
Latif:	Ooh. Oooh.

Kenya: *(Roars like a monster)*
Squirt: Oh the monster, the monster.
Latif: Oh.
Kenya: *(Roars)*
Squirt: Oh he rolled in the grass.
          (Squirt and Kenya crawl to each other)
Kenya: I'm a tiger.
          Squirt you supposed to be the zookeeper and say here tig, here lion, here lion.
Squirt: Here lion. Here, lion.
Kenya: You sposed to give me food.
Squirt: You want a big gigantic bone, Lion?
Kenya: Squirt then you sposed to come over here and let me out and I sposed to get out to people and you didn't know that I stealed the key. You sposed to be turned around talking and I got the keys and sposed to be gone.
          You sposed to say "How did you get out here?"
          Squirt pretend you sposed to pat me and to make me go to sleep and you sposed to drag me over to my place.

As in the previous example there is an expert and a novice. Kenya dominates this interaction, telling poor Squirt what he is to do. But all three children in this episode are having a wonderful time. Even the 2-year-old finds the whole drama exciting. The actual talk activity in this topic takes up almost the entire 40 minutes, with none of the children tiring of the antics of this monster-creature created by Kenya. This kind of guided participation captured the interest of both a 6-year-old and a 2-year-old at the same time. The sense of drama and theater created by the children can only really be appreciated when you are there listening and watching the major actors take the challenge of keeping the others involved in the storyline and the images created.

Both of these are examples of participatory storytelling where the action of the individuals is paired with the imaginative language in a way that evokes the richness of their language and captures the interest of others. This kind of imaginative talk is much less likely to occur in the context of adult/child interaction where adults would not so easily become captivated by the child-like images. In public school, participatory story-telling with another child is almost never encouraged because of the emphasis on individual achievement. It is hard to imagine schools that would encourage the creation of stories through joint effort of older and younger children.

Although there was certainly some complex imaginative play in the Mainstream group, the quality of the play was not as high because it generally did not involve a complex narrative sequence. This Mainstream pretend play involved much role-playing but the level of imagination and the richness of images was in striking contrast to what we had seen in the neighborhoods of the Abecedarian children. The following example was particularly representative of 5-year-old Mainstream girls who were often found playing "Barbies" or paper dolls together. Unfortunately, the talk was mostly centered on what the dolls were wearing and where they were going without the richness of the descriptions we found in the Abecedarian children's talk. These three Mainstream girls are playing with Barbie dolls as well as a number of ethnic dolls dressed in the traditional garb of their country. Like the last Abecedarian example, this is a typical excerpt from an interaction with these dolls that went on to span almost the entire 40 minutes.

> *Monique – 5 years (target child)*
> *Christy – 7 years (friend)*
> *Kelly – 4 years (friend)*

Christy:	I'm France, I'm from France. This is Holland.
Kelly:	If you got the flag, then you'll get the flag. *(Each doll holds the flag of her country)*
Christy:	You are Sweden.
Monique:	I'm gonna go change my clothes again – hee hee – I like changing clothes.
Kelly:	Why?
Monique:	Because it's fun. Here I am again. I think this is the prettiest. *(She has put another outfit on Barbie)*
Kelly:	Well I think this one's the prettiest. *(Kelly picks up another doll)*
Christy:	Ooh, I hate that one.

Monique:	Ya know what I'm getting now.
Christy:	*(to Kelly)* You can like it *(Kelly's doll)* though.
Monique:	What did you want that to be – our house and your house. We can share the houses.
Christy:	I know.
Monique:	You wanna share the houses?
Kelly:	OK.
Monique:	This is going to be our house. My girl's gonna have some clothes up here in the front. This is my girl's house.
Kelly:	Well this is ours.
Monique:	Your girls, your girls.
Christy:	Kel, this'll be yours.
Kelly:	OK.
Monique:	Your girls can share it. You girls can share that house.
Christy:	OK.
Monique:	Or else one of your girls can share it with my house. Which do you want to do? Share the camper or share my house?
Christy:	We'll just share it. I'll just share the camper.
Monique:	Alright. We can share all of them if you like. My girl's clothes go under so they don't get wet from the rain. It's built like a tent.

The interesting difference between the narratives in the Mainstream neighborhoods versus the Abecedarian neighborhoods lies in the Mainstream children's preoccupation with objects, in this case dolls. They seem to be caught up in dressing and undressing the dolls and talking about what the dolls look like, rather than using them to create a drama or fantasy. These children's advantaged circumstances, including many toys and the accessories that go with them, might have inhibited their imagination since the toys themselves were so attractive.

The second example shows the highest level of pretend play seen in the Mainstream group. This dialogue takes place on the back porch of a house. The children have a large cardboard box that they pretend is a boat and sometimes a house. They have props like fishing poles that are leaning against the box to use in their pretend play. In the first short dialogue they are pretending that it is Christmas time and in the second they are fishing from a boat.

Lisa – 5 years (target child)
Elizabeth – 5 years

Lisa:	Let's go to sleep and read a book. No, let's say it's Christmas, OK?
Elizabeth:	OK.
Lisa:	I'll be Santa Claus. You go back to sleep. You have to pretend to deliver the presents. Well, you see good old persons I'm not really going to deliver anything. I'll just walk away under the Christmas tree. "Oh, good morning Darling."
Elizabeth:	Good morning.
Lisa:	How are you? Here's your presents. Okay, I'll reach them. Here. Here you go. Leave some for me.
Elizabeth:	Now, I take my morning walk in the store.
Lisa:	No, it's not, go back to sleep, it's the middle of the night.
Elizabeth:	How come you gave me my presents in the middle of the night?
Lisa:	Because that's when you wake up. Just go back to sleep I said.
Elizabeth:	Snore . . . Snore.
Lisa:	Stop that noise.

* * * * * * * * * * * * * * *

Lisa:	Pull up this one. Then close both the doors. Then pull down that one with the fishing pole sticking out. It's going to get dark in that – get dark. Okay, now just close it some more till that you only tell there's a little crack. *(Children trying to close box while inside it)* Here, I can do it. Okay, just close it until there's just a little crack.
Elizabeth:	Let me do something.
Lisa:	Okay me starting the boat – hurry up. *(Makes sound of motor boat)*
Elizabeth:	Don't start the boat yet.
Lisa:	Here, just come up. Now reach over and close the top one. Okay, just leave it like that. What'd you do? Did you use the bathroom in the boat? Did you? Well you better not.
Elizabeth:	No, not me.

This kind of pretend play is really a type of role-playing. The Christmas dialogue demonstrates the children's knowledge of "adult talk" as they are creating a culturally important event. They are role-playing about how they, as adults, would work through some of the traditional aspects of gift giving, etc. The fishing expedition is again acting out an important adult skill that Lisa has begun to learn in participation with her father. Thus, like the Abecedarian children these children are also engaging in guided participation. The difference is really in how the children capitalize on the opportunities available during these pretend play sequences. For the Abecedarian children, play with each other represents an opportunity to extend their abilities in creating imaginative fantasies that excite the people around them. They are often lyrical in their composition and the narratives seem to be the precursors of oral storytelling and dramatic performance, an activity highly valued in their culture. On the other hand the Mainstream children find pretend play with each other as an opportunity to role-play the many activities in which they will engage as adults. Because the Mainstream children are surrounded by material goods that more often dictate and lead their play activities, such as dolls with wardrobes of clothes, trains, and so on, they may focus their play in a more concrete and directed way rather than using the toys to stimulate their imaginations and storytelling ability.

Monologues. One other major difference between the Mainstream and Abecedarian children was in their use of monologues. Although both groups of children engaged in some monologues, overall these constituted only 5 percent of the language. Only about one third of the children had any monologues at all, since they were usually with other people, giving them little opportunity to do so. Of the children who did engage in monologues, we found the same trend as with the dialogues; the Abecedarian boys used time alone as an opportunity to think out loud about issues that they were concerned with. We found no Mainstream children or Abecedarian girls who produced monologues like the following examples.

> *James: Age 5 (sitting on a bench, looking up at the sky)*
> I like to know how it feels being up to the sky.
> I gotta get me an airplane and fly up to the sky, see how it looks. And then I'd look but I wouldn't look down from the

sky. I wouldn't look down or maybe I'd fall down. But I wouldn't jump out of a plane. Not without a parachute. Cause I know if I jump out of a plane without a parachute I'd be in big trouble. If I jump, if I had a parachute, I would. I'd jump right out. With the parachute I'd land safely. I won't fall on the ground. I land just like this, then I walk and go back to the plane again cause when I jump it's gonna be scary. But I hope mine don't crash. Cause if it would it's gonna be in big trouble.

Ben: Age 5 (walking in the field beside his apartment)
I had two balls in one day and they busted in one day. Then I got another ball. That didn't bust for two weeks. That day then I got a bird. That day, then in some days, wow, it died. Then I didn't have it. I didn't have nobody but my Mom and Dad, no animals, no dog. And then they go to live for 50 days and they, they going to die soon. Then I ain't goin to have no animals. They might not, some animals. If all my animals, if all my animals die I want to get something that never dies. It goin to be a snake. Or either an octopus. I don't see octopuses around here. I just see them on TV.

These monologues suggest that these African American boys were able to verbally represent their thoughts articulately through language as well as demonstrate their narrative skills in putting together a coherent story-like monologue.

The kinds of monologues the Mainstream children used were usually asides during a kickball game or self-directing comments as they rode their bikes or ran through the woods. Below are examples of typical monologues from the Mainstream children.

Billy: I can't believe they don't see I'm not on the base.
            (Billy is playing kickball)

Cecilia: Oh, I better not fall. Just hold on tight. This bike is
            too big.
            (Cecilia is riding her new bike)

In both dialogues and monologues we found the Abecedarian children producing more sophisticated dramas and fantasies than the Mainstream children. This was especially true for the Abecedarian boys. Clearly the setting of the neighborhood was one that elicited a high level of language skill from the Abecedar-

Plate 4.3 Abecedarian children of all ages played together in noncompetitive games that emphasized participation, not winning. (Photo by Jock Lauterer)

ian children. If we had sampled the traditional mother–child dyad situations at home or in the laboratory, we might have found differences favoring the Mainstream children. Choosing the context for description can be critical in the interpretation of the data, as we shall see later when we examine the school context for both groups of children.

Playing to Win and Playing to Play

Both groups of children were often observed playing games and singing, but again there were striking differences between the groups in the frequency of some of the game and song categories. Overall, the Mainstream children engaged in more competitive games than the Abecedarian children (20 percent of the time versus 8 percent of the time). On the other hand, Abecedarian children engaged in noncompetitive games and sang songs much more often than the Mainstream children (24 versus 11 percent). The Abecedarian girls were the ones who contributed to these group differences with 34 percent of their talk centered on rhyming games and singing songs. This difference clearly affected the lower amounts of talk in dialogues for the Abecedarian girls as reported earlier in this chapter.

According to Sutton-Smith and Roberts (1981), the differences in the games children play arise from the sociocultural perspective of their community. The two main perspectives, according to these authors, are "playing to win" and "playing to play." These two opposing philosophies arise not only from different world views but also from the economic circumstances of a people. Western culture certainly stresses "playing to win" and thus it is no surprise that we found more competitive games in the mainstream culture. On the other hand, the Abecedarian children were from an underclass population, economically and racially discriminated against by the mainstream culture. They, like others who have been oppressed or with scarce resources, need mutual support from one another to survive both materially and culturally. For instance, as has been described already, the Abecedarian children were not just the property of a nuclear family but the responsibility of the larger community. The Black community was bound together through support and responsibility for each other and its children; its people were not in competition with one another. In this way, they could forge alliances to protect themselves from the powerful mainstream community.

The ritualistic noncompetitive games we observed were similar to the ones Sutton-Smith described, that were prevalent in the frontier culture of mainstream America when survival was an issue. Games like jump rope and limbo were observed frequently in the neighborhoods of the Abecedarian children. These games, unlike many competitive games, could include children of widely different ages and abilities. These games provided the opportunity for children of different ages to work together for a common purpose, or at least enjoy each other no matter what the skill level of the individual participant.

We observed one game of limbo with children ranging in age from 1 to 18. Limbo is a game where music is played in the background and two people hold a long pole or stick at either end parallel to the ground. As the music plays all the participants stand in a line in front of the pole. One by one they must manage to go under the pole by leaning backwards and passing under the pole without hitting it or touching the ground. At first the pole is held high enough so everyone can easily maneuver under it. At each successive pass the pole is lowered so it eventually may only be two or three feet above the ground. Each player may have a slightly different and humorous style of getting under the pole. As can be imagined the 1-year-olds did pretty well walking under the lowered pole while the 18-year-olds had to develop quite expert skill in jumping forward while leaning back so far that the back of their heads would almost touch the ground. People in the community often stood surrounding the limbo area, clapping and laughing at the styles the children used to bend backwards and slide or jump forward in order to get under the pole. This type of game brings solidarity to a community and is a unique game in which a 1-year-old and an 18-year-old can both be challenged by and take enjoyment in. There ultimately is a winner of the game but the object is really to play rather than win.

The most popular competitive game for both groups of children was kickball. This was probably the case because it is one game in which most 5-year-old children can play successfully. Games like football and baseball require certain physical skills that most 5-year-olds have not yet mastered. The attempts we did see at playing these highly skilled and competitive games usually ended quickly because lack of skill prevented the children from executing critical parts of the game. Even with kickball, disputes over the rules of the games and violations of the rules were commonly seen. This mildly competitive game clearly led to contention, in contrast to the cooperation shown in the limbo game.

Songs of Play.   Most of the games that Abecedarian girls played were rhyming or singing games. Since these constituted 34 percent of their talk, it was clearly central to their after-school play activities. These traditional songs have their roots in African and early American life that go back hundreds of years. According to Courlander (1963), many of these ring games and play party songs may have originally come from early European-American or Anglo-American culture but were adapted by African Americans who were also steeped in songs and games in Africa. Thus, most of the ring games and play party songs have evolved as purely African American, even though the origins were in Colonial America. As Courlander notes, these songs require few material goods but often require creative use of language within the ritualized game or song:

> They [songs] require no props or equipment. Belonging to the children's world, they have their own rules of inheritance and survival. While adult society now lays great stress on change and newness in recreation and entertainment, tradition is in some ways stronger among children. It is they, not the adults who have preserved the vast reservoir of games, songs, rhymes, and nonsense patter which most grownups once knew but long since put behind them. Whereas many activities are learned by children from adults, traditional street and yard play, with its complexity of refinements, is inherited by one generation of children directly from another, with adults rarely intervening. (pp. 146–7)

Innovation was usually included as part of a song or game so that each individual who participated added their original contribution. This was represented by the creation of a new part of a song or dance. Most of these songs were about grown-up life and some contained words and sexual associations that would be taboo in some of the African American families. Thus, part of the children's interest in these songs was their slight illicit nature. The first song listed below, "Little Sally Walker," was one that Courlander documented as coming from early Colonial America. It has survived, almost word-for-word, 200 years later in the Piedmont area of North Carolina. This song-like game was for a mixed sex group, although we found very few boys playing the game. Children, mostly girls, stood in a circle around the child who was the target. This girl danced seductively as everyone sang the song; at the end of the song

the child was supposed to sashay over to someone of the opposite sex. In the groups we observed this usually did not happen
since few boys were seen participating in these games. The girls
might whisper a boy's name but he was usually not in the
group. Our transcription of the song is almost identical to
Courlander's, indicating the stability of these songs over time
and from place to place.

> *All children:*   Little Sally Walker
> Sittin in the saucer
> Ride Sally ride ride
> Wipe your weeping eyes
> Put your hand on you hip
> and let your backbone slip
> Oh, shimmy to the east
> Oh, shimmy to the west
> Shimmy to the one you love the best.

The next song includes a part that has to be individualized
by the child. The song is called "Here comes Jimmy Jackson."
In this song the refrain is sung first and then the song is individualized so that the target child needs to include some rhyming words to make it work. This kind of game/song would be
considered a great choice for learning better sound correspond-
ences and prereading skills as espoused by authorities in early
reading (Bradley & Bryant, 1985). As can be seen in the example
below Lavina, who was 5 years old, needed some help from
Samantha who was 9 years old. After the first child sang her
solo she sauntered over and stood behind one of the other children and put her hands on the child's hips. After the next child
sang she went behind the first child and put her hands on the
first child's hips, so that after the last child in the group sang
they had made a long chain of children who sang all together.
The refrain was sung first by the whole group and then each
child sang a solo.

> *Lavina – 5 years (target child)*
> *Samantha – 9 years (friend)*
> *Jonathan – 6 years (friend)*

Refrain:	Here comes Jimmy Jackson
	Ridin in a car
	Ridin on the hood of an automobile
	All right Jimmy – do your stuff
	Shake it up and that's enough
	(When refrain is finished, the first girl sings verse; when finished she goes behind another girl and puts her hands on the girl's hips. Then that girl sings a verse and she goes behind first girl and puts her hands on her hips – until they make a long line of girls.)
Samantha:	My name is Samantha
(creative part)	And I'm a joy
	Shake my name is Samantha
	And I dig boys
	(Sing refrain again)
Samantha to Lavina:	Go, say "My name is Lavina"
Lavina:	They call me Vina
	Shake, I dig boys
	(Sing refrain again)
Jonathan:	My name is Jonathan
	They call me Jim boy
	They call me Jim Bob
	And I dig girls
	(All laugh. Jonathan leaves embarrassed.)

One last song that was quite frequently heard was called "Shake it Seniorita." In this song the child in the middle of the group dances during the song, showing her underwear if she is wearing a dress and turning round and round. Sometimes the children would turn around until they fell on the ground laughing.

	One person in middle of circle, all sing (shimmy during refrain).
1st verse:	I wish I had a nickel
	I wish I had a dime
	I wish I had a boyfriend
	that kissed me all the time
	(Children forget words and hum)
	One day I found a man
	To kiss me all the time

Refrain: Shake it seniorita
                Shake it if you can
                Show all the boys around your block
                to see your underwear (Ooh)
                Shake it to the bottom
                Shake it to the top
                turn around and turn around,
                until you make it stop.

2nd verse: I went to Kentucky
                I went to the fair
                I followed the seniorita
                with the flowers in her hair
Repeat refrain

Not only can we view these song games as communal and noncompetitive but the guided participation of the younger children by the older ones can be seen through these rhymes and dances. Participation in these games helped strengthen the ties the children had to their past roots and to some of the traditions in the present. Courlander (1963) reported that many of these songs and dances have disappeared from the culture of the cities and the more modern elements of the country, but they were alive and well in the Abecedarian community of Milltown.

> The best place to find ring games in the South today is probably in the rural or semi-rural schoolyard where recent innovations in recreation have not yet intruded. But more and more the rural schoolhouse, even in the most isolated region, is stressing "modern" forms of play – athletic competition, "constructive" activities, and "organized" fun – and soft ball, basketball, field hockey, and athletic events are more likely to be seen than ring games. (p. 148)

Overall the Abecedarian children involved themselves in more noncompetitive games, but the girls especially played these song and dancing games that distinguished their play from the Mainstream group. As in the quantitative analyses of the children's language in the neighborhood, the Mainstream boys and girls were quite similar in the games they played and the activities in which they participated. This was not true of the Abecedarian children. We found the Abecedarian boys more involved in creating verbal fantasies and dramas while the girls more often participated in songs, dances, and rhyming games. The guided participation in these activities reflected the values and needs of the culture, with the Abecedarian children playing more cooperative games and the Mainstream children playing more competitive individualistic games.

School Talk

The category of "school talk" was a natural category of interest because we wanted to better understand children's thoughts and interpretation through the transition to public school. Surprisingly, fewer Mainstream children than Abecedarian children talked about school. Forty percent of the Abecedarian children made some mention of school during the neighborhood session while only 28 percent of the Mainstream children mentioned school. Unfortunately, neither group of children made unqualified positive comments about their school experience. Abecedarian children created monologues and dialogues about school that represented their disillusionment and sense of failure about the future, even after the first few months in school. We were really struck by the already fatalistic attitudes of these young children. There were no clearly optimistic and/or positive episodes about school.

The Mainstream children presented fairly neutral accounts of the school experience. They were more likely to reenact sequences of behavior in school, imitating children and teachers. They seemed more resigned about the experience, describing and imitating school routines.

The following example of two Mainstream children playing school does not reveal a real love of learning, only a knowledge about the "rules of the game." Arlene and Daniel are both in kindergarten. They are sitting on the back deck with Arlene's dog Zero and a host of toys, books, and a record player. Daniel is playing with a toy cash register. Arlene has the book *Black Beauty*, as well as a record containing the story that can be played while looking at the book. Arlene is desperately trying to get Daniel to do what she, the pretend teacher, wants.

She uses "teacher talk" during a pretend bookreading session at circle time. Circle time in American schools is a time when the children and teacher sit on the floor in a circle. It is often a time when the teacher reads a story to the children. The "tape" that Arlene refers to is the tape that teachers often have put on the floor or rug that marks where each child should sit at circle time.

Arlene – 5 years
Daniel – 5½ years (friend)

	Children are sitting on the back deck with dog Zero.
Arlene:	Daniel, would you go sit someplace where the tape is. Sit on the tape.
	(Daniel is still playing with toy cash register)
Arlene:	*(More insistently)* Daniel! Would you come sit in the middle of the room, please?
	Would you come sit – Would you like to hear a story about a horse?
Daniel:	Yes.
Arlene:	You wanna, you wanna hear a story about a horse? Want to?
Daniel:	Um well, let's see. Where's Zero?
Arlene:	Daniel, can you go sit on the brown tape? Daniel!
Daniel:	No. Wait. I'm trying to find Zero.
Arlene:	Zero's not in this.
	Zero's not in this.
	Now watch this.
	(Arlene opens the book and turns it so her invisible audience can see the pictures as a teacher would do in class)
Daniel:	Don't you want Zero?
Arlene:	Quit it Daniel.
	Daniel! Daniel!
	Come on.
Daniel:	Here's the daily report.
	(From cash register)
Arlene:	Daniel would you go sit on the brown tape somewhere – on the brown tape. Good. Now I can start the story of the little horse.
	Here's Black Beauty.

> *(Puts record player on and child holds up book as voice from record player is heard reciting the words in the book)*
> *(Daniel squirms and giggles)*

Arlene: Daniel don't do that please. Please.
Daniel. Please.
Daniel.

Daniel: Wanna play school?

Arlene: Yeah. That's what we *are* playing. I'm trying to read to you a story.

Arlene was not very successful in getting Daniel interested in playing school. Her "teacher talk" may remind us all of teachers we knew who were not particularly effective in getting the children interested in school. Arlene's modeling of teacher and student behavior reflected her view of how teacher and student negotiate the schooling experience.

The Abecedarian children did not talk about school extensively either. There were not many long conversations about school but the ones we found reflected a consistent pattern of disappointment in the public school experience. There were two basic themes that we identified in almost all of the talk by the Abecedarian children about their school experience. These were conflict between their hopes of success in school and their disappointment and sense of failure about their real experiences in school. As we noted earlier, the families of the Abecedarian children valued education and saw their children's future linked to progress through school. Thus the children must have experienced considerable anguish over their feelings of failure so early in the schooling process. The following two short vignettes are poignant examples of the struggles and fears that were reflected in their talk to themselves and others.

In the first example, Chad was really talking to himself, although his grandmother was sitting close by. He had just had a difficult day at school and was trying hard to make himself feel more positive about his work in school. It was clear he wanted to do well in school but was anxious about his performance.

Chad – 5 years
I was glad when I came back home. I don't like to go to school.
Cause, cause we always have to do the hard hard work. But I

got some right. I got it good right. I got it right but we have
to do hard work. I had to do it so I had to do it, so I did it.
I did every bit.

The next conversation took place on a large playground connected to a new low-income housing project where Melvin lives.
Melvin has been playing there alone for a while when an older
boy of about 16 years of age stops to talk for a few minutes.
Melvin is gently rocking back and forth on a metal rocking
horse when the older boy comes and sits beside him on a
wooden bench.

> *Adolescent boy – 16 years*
> *Melvin – 5 years*

Adolescent: You live here with your Mother?
Melvin: Yeah, I'm not kidding.
Adolescent: Say again where you'd go.
Melvin: Frank Porter Graham. *(for preschool)*
Adolescent: Like it down there?
Melvin: Naw. I go to Estes Hills.
Adolescent: Do you like it down there?
Melvin: No.
Adolescent: Do you like school?
Melvin: No.
Adolescent: What you hate about school?
Melvin: Nothin.
Adolescent: Huh?
Melvin: Nothin.
Adolescent: What you like? You gotta like something.
              Do you like school at all?
Melvin: No.
Adolescent: Are you glad you started school?
Melvin: Yeah.
Adolescent: Do you like *goin* to school?
Melvin: Huh?
Adolescent: You like goin to school, right?
Melvin: No.
Adolescent: You don't?
Melvin: No.
Adolescent: When you begin you'll like that school but I never
              liked goin to school.

Melvin:	Huh?
Adolescent:	You'll never goin to like goin to school.
Melvin:	Un un.
Adolescent:	See Melvin, you stop likin to go to school when you get there.

Conversations like these may have been rare but their significance for understanding our children's experience of school was considerable. Even in these two short vignettes, there was a feeling that the children should have liked school but they did not. This sense that they should do well in school is surely derived from the strong commitment by the Black family and the church that school was the avenue to success for African Americans. Yet, there were many barriers within the integrated schools that made these children feel a sense of future failure in the system.

Neighborhood and School Language

Although we did not have comparable data of peer language at school and in the neighborhood, we did examine teachers' ratings of children's language use in the classroom and related these to language measures in the neighborhood. We were interested in whether children who talked the most and in the most complicated ways in the neighborhood would be the ones rated by their teachers as the most adept language users in school. Labov (1972) had found that in his small sample of Black teenage boys in Philadelphia, there was no relationship between the way they used language on the street corner and how they used their language in school. Their language on the street corner was complex and thoughtful while they seemed almost completely inarticulate at school. Similarly, Tizard and Hughes (1984) found little relationship between the way young working-class girls in Britain used language at school and language at home. We wanted to see if we might find a similar trend with our children as they made the transition to school at age 5.

In the fall of the children's kindergarten year all teachers were asked to complete a short language questionnaire, called the Adaptive Language Inventory (ALI) (Feagans, Fendt, & Farran, 1995). This questionnaire contained 18 items forming six scales. The six scales were developed to examine children's use of language in conversations and narratives. *Comprehension* tapped children's understanding of stories and narratives and *Production* tapped the verbal expression of such stories and narratives. *Rephrase* referred to the ability to rephrase a communication that had not been initially interpreted correctly by the listener. *Spontaneity* referred to how often the child was able to initiate talk freely, while *Fluency* referred to the clarity and smoothness of the speech. *Listening* was really a scale to tap "attention" to language especially when the teacher was talking. In addition to these scales total IQ, as measured by the WPPSI (Wechsler, 1967) at 60 months of age for both groups, was also used.

When we correlated some of the ALI subscales and IQ with the quantitative measures in the neighborhood, we found support for Labov's findings in these 5-year-olds (Feagans & Haskins, 1986). As depicted in Table 4.1, the pattern of relationship was different for the two groups. None of the significant correlations were similar for the two groups. The general pattern for the Mainstream group supported other studies, indicating positive relationships between the ALI and IQ with Mean Length of Utterance (MLU) and a negative relationship with concrete topics. This pattern of relationship did not hold for the Abecedarian sample. There seemed to be little systematic relationship across the neighborhood language measures and the teacher ratings. Across the two groups there were 12 significant correlations. A comparison between the groups on these correlations revealed that 11 of the 12 were at least marginally significantly different from each other ($p < .1$) and five of these 11 were significantly different from each other ($p < .05$). This merely underscored the differences in the pattern of relationship between the two settings for the two groups. Although the numbers were very small when we divided the groups by sex, the correlations were even more different when we compared Abecedarian boys to the Mainstream boys. There were many negative correlations between the measures of the Abecedarian boys' talk in the neighborhood and the ratings of

Table 4.1 Correlation of Naturalistic Language with Language in School and Cognitive Status

Neighborhood language measures	Teacher ratings of language						IQ	
	Comprehension		Production		Rephrase			
	ABC	MS	ABC	MS	ABC	MS	ABC	MS
Participants	.44*	-.17	.35	-.01	.38	-.02	.21	-.23
Total words	-.04	.23	-.04	.24	.05	.21	.15	.21
Complex utterances	.22	.32	.28	.28	.37	.17	.04	.38
Imperatives	-.53*	.27	-.40	.12	-.46*	.31	-.30	.08
Questions	-.10	-.02	.00	.06	-.05	-.18	-.07	.20
Elliptical	.43*	-.16	.44*	-.22	.49*	-.06	.26	-.24
MLU	-.07	.58**	.01	.54*	-.04	.46*	.02	.48***
Concrete topics	-.03	-.38	.03	-.52*	-.04	-.55*	.00	-.28

*p < .05. **p < .01. ***p < .001.

their language in the classroom. This was reminiscent of the relationship Labov (1972) found between street language and school language in adolescent boys.

Language Use in the Neighborhood: Its Place in the Children's Lives

The data from our neighborhood observations revealed interesting insights into the lives of the children. The data suggest that all children engaged in interesting play and interactions in their neighborhoods. They talked a lot and with many different people. Siblings represented a large percentage of talk and this talk was rather sophisticated. Most children talked in sophisticated and complex ways about their lives. The Mainstream children were somewhat restricted in the range of conversations in which they engaged because they generally talked to fewer people and with children who were quite close to their own age. The Abecedarian children talked with significantly more people during the sessions and with children ranging in age from 1 to 18. Even with these differences in the setting and the large economic gulf that separated the children's lives, the quantitative language differences were not particularly impressive. All children talked mostly about concrete events and present activities. The only group difference that was significant was the enormous quantity of talk that characterized the Black boys in comparison to the Black girls, the Mainstream boys, and the Mainstream girls.

The important differences between the groups seemed to emerge in the more qualitative analyses of the content of the children's talk and its function within the sociocultural context of the community. The Abecedarian children more often engaged in dramatic play and storytelling that displayed creative language not seen in the Mainstream group. This difference probably reflected the differences not only in the kinds of settings but also in the material goods available to the children. The Mainstream children's topics of talk were somewhat driven by the toys and material goods available to them. Thus their talk often centered on describing or manipulating Barbie dolls, bicycles, board games, and so on, while the Abecedarian children were forced to use their imaginations to create images and materials in their play.

Children in the Mainstream culture participated in competitive games like baseball, football, and board games. They also seemed focused on the material goods and toys at hand in role-playing adult activities. The Abecedarian children, and especially the girls, participated in cooperative and rhyming/singing games that forged alliances among children of various ages and allowed participation by children of very different ages. The limbo game was a good example of the kind of games these children played where the object was not to win but to engage children of different ages in an organized fun activity.

Talk of school was not frequent but when it did occur it differentiated the two groups of children quite dramatically. Children in the Mainstream group were often seen modeling the behavior they saw in school or describing an event at school in a very matter of fact manner. The Abecedarian children talked about school in a disheartened, impassioned way that reflected the disappointment they felt in themselves about how they were negotiating the school experience after only a few short months in school. This usually was communicated in monologues or in short exchanges among friends or with older children.

For both groups, talk with siblings revealed the most developed abilities to engage in conversations that included conflict and its resolution. We were surprised to find little aggression in any of the children and especially among siblings in either group. Rather, we found children's abilities to manipulate one another and to successfully negotiate conflict at a highly complex level. Siblings were almost universally present for all children in the study and they seemed to stimulate a high level of language skill.

Finally, the language that we measured in the neighborhood correlated well with how teachers rated the children's language at school for the Mainstream group but not for the Abecedarian group. In fact many of the correlations between the groups were significantly different. Thus, as in Labov (1969) and others, the Abecedarian children who used language in sophisticated ways in the neighborhood were not rated as sophisticated language users by teachers at school.

In the next chapters we will try to understand better the school experiences of both the Mainstream and the Abecedarian children to see if we can explain these different relationships between neighborhood and school language use for the two groups of children. In addition, we wanted to explore how the schools might or might not capitalize on the children's home community experiences in the school setting, in hopes of understanding the Abecedarian children's sense of disappointment and failure about the transition to school.

Summary

Chapter 4 described children's talk after school in their neighborhoods. This talk was audiotaped in 40-minute sessions wherever the children played. The transcriptions of the dialogues among children and adults were coded and analyzed quantitatively and qualitatively to examine the amount and complexity of their talk.

Even though there were clear material differences between the Abecedarian group and the Mainstream group, almost all children had adequate space, toys, and playmates. The Abecedarian children played with more children and with children of different ages while the Mainstream children tended to play with fewer children and with children their own age or a sibling close in age.

The structural analysis of children's talk showed no real differences between the two groups in complexity of utterances, length of dialogues, and total talk. There was an interaction between sex and amount of talk, with Black boys talking much more than any of the other three groups.

The analysis of the topics children discussed focussed on Sibling Rivalry, Pretend Play/Storytelling, Playing to Win versus Playing to Play, and School Talk. These four themes captured about 60 percent of the talk in the neighborhood. The analysis indicated that both groups appeared to use complicated language with siblings in teasing and competing with one another. The Abecedarian children displayed a greater ability to create imaginative stories with each other in joint storytelling and in extended narrative monologues. We saw little of this kind of language use in the Mainstream children. Mainstream children participated in many more competitive games than the Abecedarian children. This translated into playing different kinds of games. Abecedarian children played more games that included children of different ages, such as limbo: These games had the goal of participation, not of winning. The Abecedarian girls were often seen in rhyming and singing games that had been handed down from generation to generation. The Mainstream children were more likely to be seen playing baseball or other traditional competitive games or playing with toys like Lego or dolls. Children's talk about school also differentiated the groups, with the Mainstream children using fairly neutral talk about school and the Abecedarian children using discouraging monologues and dialogues to express their experience about the transition to school.

Overall, both groups of children played freely with others after school and displayed complex use of language. The major differences between the groups appeared to be in the topics of their talk with respect to storytelling, competitive games, and school.

5
Learning in Small Groups: The Core of the Curriculum

The most successful classrooms may be those in which teachers succeed in creating commonly shared goals and individuals cooperate in ensuring each person's success in achieving them. The ultimate criterion becomes group accomplishment of individual progress. But this would be countervailing to prevailing practice, at least as revealed by our data.

Goodlad, 1984, p. 109

For all children, entering formal school is an enormous life transition, perhaps the most momentous of their young lives. Although children from all backgrounds and ability levels enter public school in the United States at the same age, the experience of schooling by these children from diverse backgrounds can be very different. This major transition and the children's subsequent adjustment to school sets the stage for the rest of the children's educational career. Alexander, Entwisle, and Dauber (1993) have persuasively argued from their large longitudinal study in Baltimore, Maryland that children who have fallen behind and feel alienated from school in kindergarten and first grade rarely recover academically, even if intellectually they have come to school on an equal footing with their peers.

This early experience of failure in school has been more characteristic of minority children and children who come from families with less knowledge of the "middle-class" values espoused in schools. The importance of this early sense of failure by children has been supported by a number of investigations of the academic trajectories of different groups of children (Goodlad, 1984; Tizard & Hughes, 1984).

There are also a number of studies in the United States that have provided early intervention to poor children in order to prepare them better to meet the expectations of the public school. A review of the effects of these early intervention studies (Lazar et al., 1982) indicated that many of the programs produced initial academic gains that washed out by around the third year in school. They did produce fewer instances of repeated grades (retention) and placement in special education programs, but there were few clues in these studies of the mechanisms that may have led to the decreased effect of the early interventions over the first few years in public school.

In the present study, we were interested not only in whether our Abecedarian intervention children would thrive in public school but in the possible mechanisms within the classroom that might enhance or impede their transition to the public education system. Although our intervention children had an excellent preschool experience, they, along with the control group children, were Black and low-income entering an integrated school system where the Whites were generally educated and affluent. It was not clear whether our intervention could buffer these children from the perils of school.

In this chapter we will explore what occurred in small group activities in kindergarten and second grade for the Abecedarian children and for the Mainstream children. These small groups, usually formed by the teachers' judgments about the children's ability and their skill in reading, have often been considered the central place for intensive academic instruction in the first few years of school (Goodlad, 1984). Thus, children of similar ability and skill are grouped together for instructional purposes. The activities in these groups reflected what the teacher perceived as the important concepts in the curriculum as well as the teacher's style of communicating these concepts to the children. Although initially we were interested in whether the Abecedarian intervention and non-intervention children differed in the small groups in the classroom, it was clear from our initial data collection, as well as from our later analyses, that the intervention had not really affected what happened to the children in the classroom. Thus this chapter will describe more generally how children from the mainstream differed from the Abecedarian children during small group instruction.

We began collecting intensive observational teacher/child interaction data on the latter half of the Abecedarian children who entered school. This included data on about 40 Abecedarian children who were seen in kindergarten and second grade. We also collected data on the comparison Mainstream children in the same classrooms as our Abecedarian children. As mentioned previously, these comparison children were randomly selected from children of the same sex and classroom as our Abecedarian children. We were especially interested in trying to understand whether different kinds of information were being transmitted to the children in the different ability groups as well as how the styles of the teachers differed by ability group. Since our children were minority children, we were also interested in how they might be treated in comparison to the more mainstream White children.

The Classrooms

When we began this project, we were surprised by the enthusiastic participation of most of the teachers. We met with each of them, taking notes on their philosophies of teaching and the ways in which they structured their classrooms for learning. We also asked about the number and kinds of different children in the classrooms and other relevant descriptive information. We obtained permission to take pictures of their classrooms as well as to draw a floor plan of the classrooms. In addition, pictures were taken of the small groups (usually ability-grouped) in the location where they met in the classroom.

The schools had changed in many ways from the somewhat dreary colorless classrooms I remember in elementary school during the 1950s in the United States. Especially noticeable was the change in the physical characteristics of the classrooms that

Plate 5.1 Kindergarten class with teacher and reading aide. (Photo by Barbara Tyroler)

reflected their more informal and inviting nature. These class-rooms were all very bright and cheery with colorful materials displayed almost everywhere in the rooms. Most of these schools had been built since 1960 and the classrooms had many windows as well as their own door to the outside. Some of the schools had originally been designed to have open classrooms with little or no walls between the rooms. This had been modified over the years so that all classrooms we visited were self-contained with a modicum of privacy and quiet from other classrooms. This was especially true of the kindergarten classrooms. None of these kindergarten classrooms contained desks but all had tables, usually round, that seated four to six students. The classrooms had an informal, almost home-like atmosphere. Many of the teachers had set up a corner of the room with a rocking chair or at least with a throw rug and pillows for informal reading or looking at books. Most of the classrooms also had "center" areas where specific materials were placed for use by the children at certain times of the day. These centers were used to foster skills or to introduce new material. For instance, all classrooms contained a science center which was located in

Plate 5.2   Kindergarten small groups. (Photos by Barbara Tyroler)

a particular area of the room. Center themes changed throughout the school year and ranged from topics such as plants to electricity to pets.

In one kindergarten classroom there was a building block area where attractive wooden blocks were stored and where

Plate 5.3   Second grade class with teacher and reading aide and crisis aide for child with disability. (Photo by Barbara Tyroler)

valued constructions built by individual children were labeled "Do Not Touch." At another corner of the room was a bead center which included many different types of colorful beads and instructions on how to make different patterns as well as ideas on how to develop creative new patterns. The science center was actually situated in the middle of the classroom with live plants and an attractive gerbil homestead in which the animal could race through tunnels and mazes. Additional centers could be set up in the room depending on the activity of the day. For instance, the art center contained basic materials but the directions for use of these materials changed almost daily.

Children in these kindergarten classrooms had what was called "center time" when they actually could have some level of choice in deciding in which center to play. There was large variability among the teachers in how free the children were to choose any center as well as in how much of the day was allocated to spending time at these centers. As one might imagine, some of these classrooms appeared quiet and well organized, even with the variety of activities available to these kindergarten children. In other classrooms teachers allowed what we came

Plate 5.4 Second grade small groups. (Photos by Barbara Tyroler)

to call organized chaos, with children talking and joking and often creating such havoc that the observers, along with their equipment, were presented with the challenge of trying to observe and record these children as they leap-frogged from one area within the classroom to the next.

The bulletin boards that often lined the classroom walls were filled with both educational information about the topics being discussed in the classroom and examples of student products. These bulletin boards were universally very colorful and attractive, reflecting the time it must have taken to construct them. Even the ceilings were used for curricular purposes. Almost every classroom had mobiles hanging from points all over the ceiling and one classroom ceiling was painted to look like a nighttime sky. These stimuli engaged the interest of the children and reinforced the themes that the teacher was currently emphasizing in the classroom.

Although many of the second grade classrooms were also informal in nature, most of them contained movable desks that were scattered around the room, interspersed with tables. Some teachers chose to cluster three or four desks together to form one large table or work group. Yet, every second grade classroom also had an informal area where small reading and work groups could meet with the teacher about specific topics. As in the kindergarten classrooms, these areas usually contained chairs and/or a throw rug where students could sit comfortably.

Although most second grade classrooms had science and art centers these areas tended to be at the back of the room and were not as visible as those in the kindergarten classrooms. By this grade level, the wall space also contained large expanses of chalkboards for the teacher and students to use for instructional purposes.

Thus, both the kindergarten and second grade classrooms were clearly designed to attract the interest of young children and to create a comfortable atmosphere for learning. We were all impressed by the efforts that the teachers had expended in creating these environments for the children in their classroom, often using much of their own personal property and resources to make the classroom reflect their own teaching personality.

Structural Information about Classrooms

Teachers and Children

The number of children in each classroom ranged from 23 to 29 with an average of 25.8 children per class. All classes contained a teacher's aide, who was trained as a reading specialist, in accordance with a North Carolina law that mandated that such a specialist be present in every elementary classroom. Approximately 20 percent of the teachers were African American while the rest were Caucasian.

Composition of the Small Groups

These small groups were composed of three to 13 children with a mean of 6.8 children per group. The groups were constituted through teacher observation of the children's work and through standardized test results. All teachers used the groups for both the teaching of new concepts and for drill and practice. They also all used the groups for teaching reading and language arts. Only seven teachers taught math in these groups.

Although these groups had value-free names like "Blue Birds" and "Robins," most kindergarten teachers reported that they grouped children together because of similar skill levels. Most teachers had a minimum of three skill groups but some had as many as six. In kindergarten 40 percent of the teachers said they did not group children together by ability or skill but rather tried to balance the groups.

By second grade all teachers grouped children by ability. Teachers reported that children moved from one group to another as their skills improved or deteriorated. This flexible principle seemed reasonable in theory but in practice the children we were studying almost never moved to another skill group. Thus, once placed in a low-ability group, children tended to stay in that group throughout the school year.

Teachers met with these different ability groups on an average of four to five times per week. In kindergarten the small group time ranged from 45 to 150 minutes per week, with an average of 88.5 minutes per week. Second grade ability groups met from 60 to 150 minutes per week with an average of 80.2 minutes per week. Thus, although there was great variability in the length of time the groups from each classroom met per week, the mean time for kindergarten and second grade was remarkably similar.

The Abecedarian children, both experimental and control, tended to be placed in the lower ability groups in comparison

Table 5.1   Ability Group Membership by Group and Grade[1]

	Kindergarten[2]		
	High group %	*Medium group* %	*Low group* %
Abecedarian group	5.9	60.0	35.3
Mainstream group	52.9	41.2	5.9
	Second grade		
	High group %	*Medium group* %	*Low group* %
Abecedarian group	5.9	35.2	58.9
Mainstream group	41.2	53.0	5.9

[1] Chi squares for both grades: $p < .01$.
[2] There were 13 children in each group who were in classrooms where the teacher did not group by ability. These children are not reflected in the table. All classrooms in second grade used ability groups.

to the Mainstream children at both grade levels. In kindergarten only 6 percent of the Abecedarian children were in high-ability groups while 60 percent were in medium groups and 35 percent in low groups. By second grade the trend was even more discouraging with 6 percent of our children in the high groups, 35 percent in the medium groups and 59 percent in the low groups. This same trend was not evident for the comparison Mainstream children. In fact, the trend was just the opposite with most of them in the high or medium groups in kindergarten and second grade. By second grade the differences were even more striking with well over half of the Abecedarian children in the lowest group and almost all of the comparison Mainstream children in the two highest groups.

Table 5.1 shows how the Abecedarian children compared to the Mainstream children with respect to ability group membership. Because teachers told us that the most concentrated teaching took place within these groups, and because the Abecedarian children, both experimental and control, were most often in the lower ability groups, it was important to understand how these groups operated and what kind of information was being conveyed. Interviews with teachers gave us some basic information about these groups and we then observed them on two different occasions to assess more systematically the teachers' and the children's behavior and to record the language interactions in these small groups.

Although evidence has amassed that these ability groups do not facilitate learning for the children in the lower ability groups (Goodlad, 1984; Entwisle et al., 1987), teachers appeared to persist in using them. Teachers reported to us that they believed better instruction could be given in the ability groups because the lesson could be geared more to the individual level of the child. They also believed that these groups allowed the extra time necessary for those who needed more practice with a lesson. The teachers reported to us that they were communicating the same information to all groups but that different strategies and time frames were needed for different ability groups. Teachers also told us that management problems in the lower ability groups often interfered with students' learning and that, by grouping children by ability, a higher quality of instruction could be sustained.

We wanted to actually document whether the teachers' perceptions were borne out by systematic observation of the children and teachers. We wanted to understand whether effective teaching strategies were being employed in ability groups and if this practice might not actually be as damaging as has been reported in the literature. On the other hand, if the teachers were misperceiving their instructional styles and content, we hoped to understand why.

Much of the information on ability group placement has come from studies of older children who are commonly placed in tracks for instruction in junior high schools (12-, 13-, and 14-year-olds) and beyond. For instance, most schools after elementary school in the United States have one or two "tracks" for students who plan to go on to college and other "tracks" for what are called vocational students, not planning to go on to a four-year college course. Students are segregated within the school, having different teachers and different content in the classes. In a recent study of tracking in junior high school, Goodlad (1984) concluded:

> High track classes spent a larger proportion of class time on instruction and their teachers expected students to spend more time learning at home than was the case in the low tracks. High track classes devoted more time to relatively high level cognitive processes, making judgments, drawing inferences, effecting syntheses, using symbolism, and so on. Low track classes devoted a much larger share of instructional time to rote learning and the application of knowledge and skills. Again, the middle track classes were more like the upper than the lower track classes. (p. 154)

Although there seems to be convincing evidence that "tracking" is not beneficial to the students in the lower tracks in junior high school and beyond, it is not clear whether the ability groups in elementary school would yield the same negative findings.

The Procedure for Observing Children in Small Group Sessions

In order to gather the information we needed about the small groups we asked each of the children in the study to wear a vest that contained a wireless microphone during their small group sessions. Many of these children had worn such a vest previously during our neighborhood observations and were familiar with how it worked. These veterans were often used as models for the other children in the class who were more uncomfortable wearing the vest; however, in almost all cases the children gladly wore it. In the few cases where children refused to wear one, even after several attempts, we allowed them to hold it or lay it next to them during the small group session.

The language in the small group was recorded by an observer sitting near the receiver and tape recorder. The observer also took extensive contextual notes to allow clearer interpretation of the transcriptions. In addition, a second observer was recording the children's behavior in the small group using a time sampling procedure that categorized the children's and teacher's task behavior in five-second intervals. During the observation, information was also obtained about the content of the lessons that were being observed.

The observations in the small groups were done on two separate days. Although there was wide variation in the amount of time teachers met with the small groups (see numbers above), they met with the low, medium, and high groups for the same amounts of time. This did not coincide with the teachers' perceptions that they met for longer periods of time with the low-ability groups. The discrepancy between the teachers' perceptions and our observations may have been because we observed the groups on only two separate occasions. Thus, from our observations we found no evidence that low-ability children were getting more small group time.

Observations in the Small Groups

Information that was obtained through our observational system was designed to provide a picture of the teacher and child during small group instruction. There were six different target activities that were coded every five seconds in the small groups. These included: (1) the content of the small activities, (2) the nature of the task requirements, (3) the teachers' strategies during instruction, (4) the teachers' use of language during instruction, (5) the child's attending behavior during instruction, and (6) the child's talk during instruction. Each of these target activities will be discussed in turn.

Activities in the Small Groups

Much of the instruction that goes on in elementary classrooms takes place in small teacher-led groups. Here, the core of the key elements of reading and math are often first explored in depth. It is in this context that most of the interaction between

Table 5.2   Summary of Content of Small Group Activities

Activities	Percentage in kindergarten	Percentage in second grade
Reading	46	95
Oral language	23	
Writing	11	
Math, logical thinking	10	5
Drawing, scissors, pasting	8	
Unclassified	2	

teacher and child can theoretically take place because the group is smaller and the atmosphere somewhat less formal.

Besides the information that teachers provided about the content of the small groups, the curricular activities of the small groups were recorded every five seconds in each of the observed small group sessions. These data are summarized in Table 5.2.

In general, the kindergarten teachers used the small group settings for a more varied set of teaching experiences, including a number of reading and writing skills, math, fine motor skills, and even worksheets. This varied use of the small groups may have been necessary because as children enter public school they need a more structured situation to learn all the basic skills required for the other academic lessons. So, for instance, learning how to use scissors, pasting, and recognition of color names were all taught in the small group. These basic skills were needed for activities in both reading and math later in the school year.

The second grade activities in the small groups were almost exclusively reserved for reading activities even though we expected to see more math concepts being taught, based on our teacher interviews. Teachers in both grades reported that they did teach math in skill groups; however, we did not observe this to be the case in either grade, and especially so in second grade. Rather, worksheets and general directions written on the chalkboard seemed to be more prevalent for math instruction, at least while we were observing the classes. Teachers seemed to meet individually with students who had trouble with math concepts, rather than handling this in the small group sessions.

Teachers in the United States feel especially pressured to make sure children have good reading skills by the end of second grade. Reading is assumed to be a tool children have mastered by the third grade so that they can use this skill to acquire new knowledge in other areas of the curriculum. Thus, the textbooks used in social studies and science in third grade are ones that require children to be able to read well. It is incumbent upon second grade teachers to produce as many competent readers as possible by the end of the school year, in order to ensure a successful transition to third grade.

Demands of the Task

We also coded the demands of the task that teachers presented to the children in the small groups. These were divided into three major types. The first category was *passive attending*. This kind of task required the children to listen and attend to the teacher without active child participation required. This included teacher-focussed activities like lecturing or showing a movie. *Active participation* activities were those that required verbal responsiveness by the child in teacher/pupil interactions or pupil/pupil verbal exchanges. These activities may have included "show and tell" or question–answer sessions set up by the teacher. Thus some teacher-focussed activities may have actively encouraged children's participation and talk. *Nonverbal active* activities were those in which the child nonverbally responded to task demands. This category included activities like worksheets or the manipulation of objects that may have been provided for a science or other project in which the group was engaged.

Figure 5.1 shows that in kindergarten the tasks were evenly divided among the three categories: *passive*, *active*, and *nonverbal active*. In second grade the tasks demanded more active and less passive participation by the children.

Only about 30 percent of the kindergarten lesson time was structured so that the children sat passively and listened. In

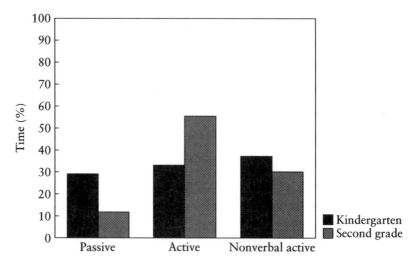

Figure 5.1   Level of Student Participation Required in Small Groups,
by Age Level

second grade it was even less, with the children passively listening 10 percent of the time. For another 30 percent of the
time in kindergarten the activities in the small groups were
set up for the children to be verbally responsive and to take an
active role in the discussion. By second grade this had risen to
55 percent of the time. Nonverbal activities, like worksheets,
took up about 30 to 35 percent of the time in both grades.

Thus it appeared that teachers attempted to structure activities so that children could participate actively in the learning.
By examining the actual amount of student participation and
teacher talk, we can assess whether the teachers were successful
in getting the children actively involved in the learning process.

Teacher Activity

The kind of format the teacher used during instruction was
coded into four mutually exclusive categories. *Teacher focus*
was a category coded when the teacher was the focal point
of the activity. This included lecturing the children, questioning them, testing their knowledge, and directing them to do an

activity. It also included activities like watching a video tape where the focus was a teacher-initiated activity. In all these activities the teacher was controlling the flow of information with minimal input from students. *Teacher participation* captured activities that were more peer-focussed and where the children themselves took the lead in the activity, with the teacher participating and stimulating the children to think. This kind of activity was similar to Rogoff's conception of guided participation and apprenticeship since the children often chose important events or activities in their lives to share with the group. The most frequent example of this format of teaching was "show and tell" where the child was the one who chose the content and the children did most of the talking. *Teacher onlooking* occurred during times when children worked independently, as might happen when worksheets are being completed. In this case, the teacher moved from child to child in the small group making sure they were able to do the work correctly and keeping children focussed on the task in hand. In addition, we coded times when the teacher was gone from the group and there was *no teacher input*. This happened if an adult visited the classroom unexpectedly or if a few children were disruptive or needed help in another part of the classroom.

Because kindergarten was more unstructured than second grade and because children there had less experience with a lecture-type format, we thought that the groups in kindergarten would contain fewer teacher-focussed activities in the small group. Our data showed this not to be the case.

Figure 5.2 indicates that teachers were the focal point of activities in the groups 70 percent of the time in kindergarten and 85 percent by second grade. We were surprised at the large amount of the time teachers lectured in these groups at both grade levels. The teacher engaged in a participatory exchange with students only 10 percent of the time in either grade. This was somewhat surprising since teachers had set up activities that allowed for more student input, as judged by the demands of the task. This was in contrast to the kinds of learning interactions we had observed in the home neighborhoods of all children where participatory learning was common.

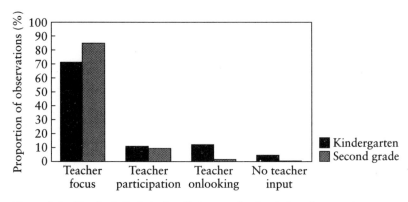

Figure 5.2   Teacher's Role in Small Groups, by Grade Level

Teacher Talk

Teachers' verbal behavior was coded every five seconds into five categories: (1) *talk directed at the target child*, (2) *talk directed to the entire small group*, (3) *talk directed to another individual child in the small group or in the larger group*, (4) *nonverbal demonstration or writing on the chalkboard*, and (5) *leaving the small group to do other work*.

Figure 5.3 depicts the proportion of time teachers talked either to the target child or to the other children in the group. In kindergarten teachers only allowed children to talk about 15 percent of the time and in second grade they allowed children to talk 25 percent of the time.

Teachers were clearly the dominant focal point for almost all activities. They appeared to set up demands in the tasks for children's active participation verbally (figure 5.1) but the teachers did almost all of the talking. Teachers talked about 75 percent of the time in the small groups, leaving little time for children's verbal participation. This reinforces the activities in which the teacher was engaged (figure 5.2).

Child Behavior

Given the kind of teaching in the small groups, we wanted to see whether teachers were able to keep children engaged in the

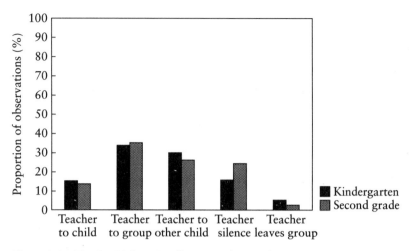

Figure 5.3 Teacher Talk in Small Groups, by Grade

task in hand. Since there was so much teacher talk and teacher-directed activity, we wanted to document whether the children were actually attending to the teacher or whatever the task was before them. This would give us some indication of how engaged the children were during learning opportunities in the small group.

We devised three categories to capture the attentiveness of the children. Every five seconds we coded whether the children were attending to the task in hand. *Passive attention* was coded when the child focussed on the teacher or the task (such as a movie) but this attention was not active, so the child was observed watching the appropriate activity. *Active attention* was coded when the child was actively engaged in an activity, such as drawing, writing, answering questions, nodding their head, and so on. *Non-attention* was coded when the child was not focussed on the task. This included daydreaming, playing with non-task objects like paper wads and little trinkets brought to school, talking to a peer during a lesson, or not doing the work assigned. It also included antics that were not appropriate for the classroom: For instance, one boy did a back flip out of his chair when the teacher was not looking. This was coded as *non-attention* even though he accomplished this antic without disrupting the group.

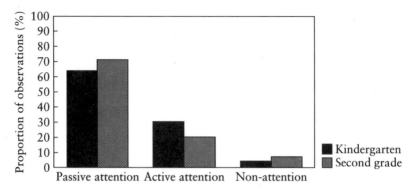

Figure 5.4　Children's Behavior in Small Groups, by Grade

Children from all groups acted appropriately in the group settings over 90 percent of the time at both grade levels, as can be seen in figure 5.4. It appeared that the teachers had excellent control of the groups so that children were engaged in the tasks, even when they were not actively participating most of the time. We found no evidence that attention was poorer in the lower ability groups. Thus, teachers were successful in keeping all children focussed on the task in hand no matter what their skill level.

Child Talk

Like those of the teachers, the children's verbal and nonverbal behaviors were also coded into categories every five seconds during the small ability group sessions. These included: (1) *talk directed to the entire small group* as in reading aloud or "show and tell," (2) *talk to peer in the group*, (3) *talk directed to the teacher*, (4) *talk directed to oneself*, and (5) *nonverbal response to the teacher or to the activity*, such as raising one's hand or other meaningful nonverbal response.

Children's talk in the small groups paralleled the results just described of the teachers' talk. Children were speaking as part of the task only about 15 percent of the time and they were silent about 70 percent of the time (see figure 5.5).

Interestingly, the children talked to themselves about 15 percent of the time. The content of this talk generally consisted of

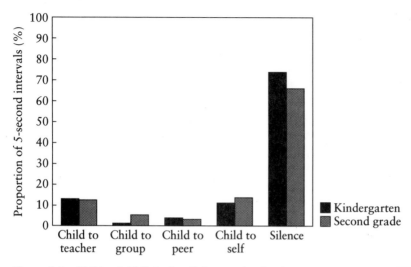

Figure 5.5   Children's Talk in Small Groups, by Grade

whispering answers to questions posed by the teacher, practicing the pronunciation of words or sounds, and making humorous asides about the work or lesson. In general, teachers did not hear this talk but we were able to pick it up because the wireless microphones were so close to the children's faces. It was also a further indication that the children were not very inhibited by the microphone or the vest.

Again, we found no group differences in child talk and really no differences by grade level either. Children were generally silent and talked to themselves about as much as they talked to the teacher at both grade levels.

High- Versus Low-Ability Groups

Besides examining grade differences, we were also very interested in comparing high- versus low-ability groups at each grade level in order to describe any differences that might be found in the way the groups operated. Surprisingly, we found no ability group differences on any of the six areas just described. Children in low- and high-ability groups seemed to be receiving the same kind of overall demands in these lessons. Teacher activities and talk also did not differentiate the groups.

There has been evidence in the literature (Haskins, Walden, & Ramey, 1983), and anecdotally from the teachers, that children in the lower ability groups were more difficult to handle and thus the reason these children were not getting the same quality of instruction was because they did not attend as well during instruction. We were very interested in whether the Abecedarian intervention and non-intervention children differed in attentiveness during small group sessions, as well as in whether these two groups differed from the Mainstream children in the same situation. When we looked for differences among the groups, we did not find any at all. As was seen in figure 5.4, all children were extremely attentive in these small groups.

The Content of Teacher and Child Talk in Small Groups

Given these similarities across grades and ability groups in the kind of teaching being done and the behavior of the children, we were really interested in whether the complexity of the content differed between grades and ability groups. Goodlad (1984) had examined junior and senior high school tracking and found that "effective instructional practices were found to be more characteristic of high than of low classes. Students in the lower tracks were the least likely to experience the types of instruction most highly associated with achievement" (p. 155). High track classes were rated as having greater teacher clarity, organization, and enthusiasm. We were interested in these and several other factors.

We took the transcripts from each of the two sessions for each child and examined the *complexity* or abstractness of the information conveyed as well as the *length of the dialogues* between the teacher and the class on a particular topic. The purpose of this latter category was to capture whether teachers could sustain a topic conversation for longer periods with students considered to have higher ability in comparison to students considered to have less ability. We also rated the *organization* and *clarity* of the lesson to assess whether the teachers were effective in their presentation of the information. These last two categories were global judgments made on each entire small group session observed. Each of the categories was rated on a five-point scale ranging from "very poor" to "excellent." *Organization* was defined by a variety of criteria including the quality of the introduction to the lesson and the sequencing of information within the lesson. *Clarity* was defined with respect to how sensitive the teacher appeared to be in the ability to gauge the level of information for her students. For instance, some teachers wandered off the point or gave rather vague instructions about what was expected of the children.

Overall, our results showed marked differences in the content of the lessons between high- and low-ability groups. In general this was also supported when we compared the ability groups containing Abecedarian children versus those with Mainstream children, although Abecedarian children were not in lower ability groups in every instance. Indeed, the children from the Mainstream were in groups where discussion on a topic (*length of the dialogue*) was almost twice as long as in the Abecedarian children's groups and fewer topics were covered during the group time. The Abecedarian children were more often in groups where there were more molecular topics and the dialogues were shorter. *Organization* and *clarity* were also rated as superior in the high-ability groups. In some ways this seemed counterintuitive since it might seem logical that it would be more difficult to structure the more complex and higher level material. That did not seem to be the case among the teachers in either kindergarten or second grade.

Kindergarten Small Groups

It might be helpful to actually see some of these dialogues to capture the differences we were observing. The following are two short instructional dialogues from two Mainstream children in kindergarten who were in medium- or high-ability groups and two children from the Abecedarian group who were in low-ability groups in kindergarten.

High-Ability Groups in Kindergarten

Example 1

Teacher	Target Child	Other Children
Why/why is he so afraid to have a doll?		
	Because he's a boy.	
Kevin?		
	Because he is a boy (_____) and, um, he doesn't want to be caught thinking, "Oh no, a boy playing with a little doll." I mean the/he thinks that it's for girls, not for boys.	
Have any of you ever played with a doll?		
	Yes. Stuffed animals (_____)	
Do you think it's so bad?		
	No.	(I don't have) (any) stuffed animals.
This story was written a very long time ago. Now I want you to {know this} {notice} This story was written a very long time ago when little boys didn't ever play with dolls.		
		Why not?
They just didn't. And now boys (-do) with dolls a lot, don't they?		

Teacher	Target Child	Other Children
	m m	Yeah.
So I'm not really sure that this same story would be written today at all.		
	m m. I doubt it.	

Example 2

Teacher	Target Child	Other Children
Alright. Another one. These are just fun. Alright, raise your hand if you think you are ready with this one. Terry?		
	[laughs]	Chubby. Kitten.
Alright. What's the synonym for chubby?		
	Fat.	Fat.
What would be a synonym for kitten that rhymes with fat?		
	Cat.	Cat.
Alright. Fat Cat.		
	[laughs]	Chubby kitten. Fat cat.
Raise your hand		
	[giggles] Chubby kitten. Fat cat. This is so funny.	[giggles]
Ssh – calm down here. Alright. Let's try another one.		
		Warm (_____).
Raise your hand. Amanda, synonym for warm.		

Teacher	Target Child	Other Children
		Hot.
Alright, synonym for place – has to rhyme with hot.		
		Sh—
You're thinking, but it has to rhyme so – it will make it exactly the same. What's this? And, you're thinking – A warm place— A hot____mmm. You're thinking. You're thinking.		
		(_____) [whisper]
Did anyone say, save a place for me? Save me that spot.		
	I didn't say (_____) (_____).	Spot.

Low-Ability Groups in Kindergarten

Example 1

Teacher	Target Child	Other Children
Find the pictures of the hammer, horse, and helicopter at the top of the card. Put your finger on each picture and say its name after me. Hammer. Hammer.		
	Hammer.	Hammer.
Horse.		
	Horse.	Horse.

Teacher	Target Child	Other Children
Helicopter.		
	Helicopter.	Helicopter.
Helicopter. Use your finger, please. Notice that hammer, horse, and helicopter begin with the same sound. Put your finger on each picture again and say each one after me. Think how each one sounds at the beginning. Hammer. Hammer.		
	Hammer.	Hammer.
Horse.		
	Horse.	Horse.
Helicopter. Helicopter.		
	Helicopter.	Helicopter.
Look at the next row of pictures and put your finger on the heart. Say heart.		

Example 2

Teacher	Target Child	Other Children
Okay, let's look at the animals, the animals that we have. Okay, Bosco the Bear and what letter does Bosco begin with, what letter, Jonathan?		
		B
B. Okay, we'll let . . . How 'bout . . . Jessica?		
	Mischief the Monkey.	
Okay, now what letter does the monkey begin with?		
	M.	
Good girl. How 'bout this one?		
		Silky the Seal.

Teacher	*Target Child*	*Other Children*
Silky the Seal. Mr. G, Mr. F.		
And what letter does		
Silky the Seal begin with?		
		S.

The two excerpts from high-ability groups underscore the fundamental difference in the quality of instruction that could not be captured by the previous description of the groups. In both the high- and low-ability groups the teacher was clearly in control of the conversation and did most of the talking, but the quality of talk in the two kinds of groups differed. In the first of these examples from the high-ability group the teacher was trying to make the children think about the issue of boys playing with dolls. This topic clearly engaged the attention and thought of the children and the style of instruction was very conversational. This kind of back and forth informal yet informative exchange was reminiscent of some of the conversations heard in the home or neighborhood setting. This kind of dialogue was extremely rare in the low-ability groups.

Example 2 from a high-ability group was a more formal learning situation but it was fun for both the teacher and children and it evolved into a rhyming game that required fairly good phonemic skills. I chose this example because we never saw such instructional rhyming games used with the low-ability groups, yet this was the type of activity we had just seen in the neighborhoods of the Abecedarian children where children were required to supply a new phrase with an ending rhyming word to rhyming verses and songs. It was unfortunate that these teachers did not have the opportunity to observe the Abecedarian children in their home community as we did. These rhyming games would have been exactly the kind of participatory activity the Abecedarian children enjoyed, but few were given the opportunity to engage in rhyming games at school.

In the low-ability groups the talk was reminiscent of many of the descriptions given by other studies examining low-ability groups. These groups more often were engaged in drill and practice with rote learning emphasized. This was not to say that the teachers were not animated and engaged, but the quality of instruction was not as high or as complex as in the high-ability groups.

The first example from the low-ability group was actually a pleasant teaching sequence, with the teacher presenting the children with colorful attractive pictures. Unfortunately, the level of teaching was rather basic and geared to factual information about reading without an effort to make the children think about the content of the language they were using.

The second example was also typical of the low-ability groups. Teachers were often engaged in helping the children with worksheets where the session was extremely structured and the children's responses were almost completely restricted by the nature of the worksheet. We saw little discussion of issues and teachers relied on preprinted and prepared materials when instructing the lower ability groups. This may have been the case because the teachers felt less confident about their skills in instructing such groups or because they felt that drill and practice was a more necessary part of the learning process for these children.

Second Grade Ability Groups

The second grade ability groups were characterized by much longer lessons and much more complex subject matter. These two changes were not very surprising. The differences between the ability groups were even more stark at second grade. The two examples of lessons from the high-ability group and the two examples from the low-ability group illustrate the differences in the complexity and organization of the lessons.

High-Ability Groups in Second Grade

Example 1

Teacher	Target Child	Other Children
Let's see if you can read the words I put on the board.		
	uphill	(group in
	downstairs	unison)

Teacher	Target Child	Other Children
Downstairs that's like going down stairs. If you're upstairs in your house you can go downstairs.		
	downstairs starlight moonlight daylight sunlight something	
Something, OK . . . Billie had the magic word for what we were gonna do this morning. We're gonna study words that are called what?		
	compound words	
Compound words. We've talked about compound words before. This is just a review really of compound words. Raise your hand if you remember what the rule is for a compound word. We talked about the rule for making compound words. Why do we call these words compound words, Jack? Not letters but words.		
		(Jack mumbles answer shyly)
Can you say that loud. You're saying it exactly right but I need everybody in this group to hear it.		

Teacher	*Target Child*	*Other Children*
		Two words put together make one word.
You're absolutely right. What did he say the rule was Vicki?		
		A compound word are two words put together to one whole word.
(Children are now asked to give new compound words.) Is there another one?		
		(John) I know one. I know one. Gas tank.
Gas tank? I think gas tank is written as two words John.		
		John (whispers word)
Say it again		
		Policeman
Policeman. That's the one you were thinking about. We say policeman but now what do we have to say, too?		
		Policelady.
Policelady or policewoman. Yes, we have to say this because ladies are also doing police work.		

Example 2

Teacher	Target Child	Other Children
Yesterday, yesterday we read two stories in our new book. What's our new book called, Sue Ann?		
		Magic Afternoon
It's called Magic Afternoon and we met a person in this book and his name is . . . Jon? (*calls on Jon*)		
	Mr. Figg	
Mr. Figg. Now, there was something special about Mr. Figg. What was special about Mr. Figg? Christopher do you know?		
		He had a – He was magic
He was magic, right.		
		He had a magic hat.
He had a magic hat. That's how he did it. That's one way he did his magic. What was something else unusual about Mr. Figg? Thea.		
		He had a um little house. He was real big too.
Was he big?		
	No.	No, he was little, little, I mean.
But you might just – I know what you're trying to describe.		

Teacher	Target Child	Other Children
		This part of him is real big and this is real little.
How could you describe him?		
		Little but no, big.
He was – what's the word I'm looking for? He was _____		
	Large	Big, large.
That's another word for how high something is.		
	Tall	
Tall, he wasn't very tall but he was very _____		
		big, fat
He was fat around.		
		He was very fat.

Low-Ability Groups in Second Grade

Example 1

Teacher	Target Child	Other Children
Now, let's see if you can figure out that compound word. Now don't anybody say anything.		
	I know.	Ooh ooh. I know.
So look at the next picture and it will give you a clue.		
	ty (whispers)	Typewriter. I've used that.

Teacher	Target Child	Other Children
You got it.		
	It is called a teletypewriter.	
Very good. You know what tele means? T E L E on a word?		
		Yeah and it says it'll tell you what to do – what the phone number is.
I was thinking about when you see a word. When you see T. E. L. E. – just think of all the words that you know that you've seen that on before.		
Don't call out, raise your hand.		
Give me a word that you've seen that on before.		
		Telephone.
Telephone. Good. That's a good one. Can you give me another word that you've seen that on?		
		Television.
Television, good		
	The teller II	Is teller II like a phone company?
Ok, what else?		
	Teller II	
Telephone, teletypewriter. Anybody get a message on a piece of paper. It's called a tele – what?		

Teacher	Target Child	Other Children
		Yeah, I saw it. tele-gram.
Right, telegram		
	Telegram	
That part of that word means far. You're getting a message from far.		
	Telephone.	
You're getting a telephone call from far. It's a far phone.		
		Hello.
Alright, let's think of some compound words, too. Look at the pictures *(picture of people in homes in daily activity)*		
	Grand-mother Babysitter Bathroom Bathbrush	

Example 2

Teacher	Target Child	Other Children
Let's open up our books to page 12. OK? All right – this time we'll review / you see it goes now to the short (I) and the short (O) words. Let's see how well you boys can read those words together as I point to them. What's the first one.		
	Big	Big
OK, you're looking at that as a B. It's a P		
	Pig	

Teacher	*Target Child*	*Other Children*
Pig		
	Sit	
	Slid	
	Win	
Wait a minute. Wait a minute. Before we go on – that's T. R. not T. I.		
	Tip	Truck
Uh Uh – try it again. What's the first one?		
		Try.
It's an I and it's only one vowel so it's going to make a short sound. A short sound		
	Trip	
Trip. That's better. OK what's this one?		
	Don't	Don't
Read it again		
	Don't	
	Oh, don't	
Watch the board. You think it's don't but what's this word H.O.T.		
	Hot	
What would D.O.T. be?		
	Dot	Dot
Dot, good Zach, Dot		
	Pot	
	Stop	
	Pond	
Pond, very good		

The differences between the teachers' structuring of activities for the second grade groups were indicated not only in the level of complexity that had differentiated the kindergarten ability groups but in two other quite striking ways too. First, teachers in the high-ability groups twice as often referred to abstract principles when explaining a lesson. This was rarely seen in the low-ability groups. In fact, in the low-ability groups the teachers more often relied on worksheets and didactic teaching practices. In addition, the organization and clarity of the lessons were rated significantly better in groups containing Mainstream as opposed to Abecedarian children.

The examples clearly illustrated some of these differences in teaching style between the high- and low-ability groups. The first example from a high-ability group and the first example from a low-ability group lesson were taken from the same teacher. In both cases the teacher was engaged in a lesson on compound words, but notice the difference between the groups in how she presented the material. In the high-ability group the teacher logically sequenced the lesson, referring to the abstract rule for compound words. She appeared in control of the lesson and was able to respond constructively to mistakes that children made. For instance, she acknowledged the answer by one child who gave the example of "gas tank" as a compound word by responding that she thought it was written as two separate words. The teacher was also able to use the lesson to address other important information without detracting from the lesson; for instance, she was able to discuss that since women were now in police work, one should say "policewoman" and "policeman," while still focussing on the topic of compound words.

On the other hand, the same teacher looked quite different when instructing the low-ability group. She introduced the topic of compound words less coherently, even though she used prepackaged worksheets with directions written on them. She did not refer to the abstract rules for combining words as she had in the high-ability group. In fact, she confused the issue of compound words by trying to explain what the prefix "tele" meant. This use of "tele", which cannot be used in a compound word, would almost surely confuse children when the lesson was supposed to be on compound words. In addition, she ignored the response of the target child who actually came up with what he thought was a good example of a "tele" word, "teller II." (This was a term used for an Automatic

Teller Machine (ATM), which at the time were new machines located outside of banks or shopping malls and used to get cash without having to write a check or go into a bank.) The teacher had another word in mind and thus ignored the child's response. Even when the teacher eventually got back to compound words, she did not make it clear to the children that the "tele" example was really not relevant to the lesson on compound words.

The other examples from the high- and low-ability groups served to illustrate the level of discussion between the two groups. Because the high group was actually able to read fairly simple books, it was probably more natural for the teacher to be able to create lessons that built in discussion of the story. In the low-ability group, the children's lesser ability to actually read words seemed to force her into a much more didactic mode. Although in many ways this didactic strategy seemed like a logical one to use, it clearly made it impossible for the low-ability group to be exposed to the higher level and more interesting discussions that occurred in the high-ability groups.

Teachers were clearly prepared for and engaged with the children in the small groups but it was apparent from our analysis that the content of the lessons in the differing ability groups varied and that this exacerbated the differences between the best and the least skilled students in the classes. These groups were formed with the best intentions and with the teachers well prepared for the instructional lessons, yet unaware of how differently they conducted the lessons in the various ability groups.

Summary

The schools that the children attended were attractive with colorfully decorated rooms, especially in the kindergarten classrooms. Class size ranged from 23 to 29 children with most classes having a part- to full-time reading aide in the classroom, along with the regular classroom teacher.

The teachers in this study conveyed new information to students most often in small groups that were generally formed by putting together children who had similar ability in a given subject area. These groups ranged in size from three to 13 children. Most small groups met for approximately 15 minutes per day.

The Abecedarian children were placed in lower ability groups in comparison to the Mainstream children at both grade levels. Because of the difference between the two groups in ability group placement we observed the teacher style and student behavior differences in the ability groups.

The behavior of the children in the two kinds of ability groups was not different with respect to the children's attention to the teacher or their participation in the group. The teachers tended to emphasize the teaching of reading in the groups with most of the talk directed by the teacher to the group.

The differences between the groups were found in the content and difficulty level of the material. The teachers were more organized and presented higher level material to the Mainstream children, who were in higher ability groups, than to the Abecedarian children, who were in lower ability groups. Examples of the talk by teachers and children in ability groups revealed that even when teachers were presenting the same material to high- and low-ability groups, the material was better organized and the feedback to students was more appropriate in the higher ability groups, where the Mainstream children were most often members. The lower ability groups, that contained almost all of the Abecedarian children, received lessons that were more disorganized and teachers tended to have poorer interactions and less helpful feedback to students.

6

Tutorial Interaction Between Teacher and Child

I walk through the long schoolroom questioning;
A kind old nun in a white hood replies;
The children learn to cipher and to sing,
To study reading-books and history,
To cut and sew, be neat in everything
In the best modern way—
William Butler Yeats, "Among School Children"

Although the small group sessions were informative about the kind of instruction children were receiving, they did not reveal very much about how teachers interacted with particular children on new or difficult material to be learned. It was rare to see one-to-one interaction of any length between teacher and child in the small groups. Since we were interested in how teachers and children negotiated learning about new information, we set up a teaching/learning situation in which the teacher asked prespecified questions about a wordless picture book. Some of these questions were easy to answer and some were very difficult. We were interested in what the teacher did when children had trouble answering the questions. Although this kind of situation was an idealized form of teaching/learning we felt it would provide a good reflection of what the teacher believed were best practices for teaching; it also gave us some information about the skill level of the children themselves as well as about how they might try to get information from teachers.

Much has been written since the 1970s on individualizing instruction and the kinds of strategies that teachers might use to help children progress. Joan Tough (1982) talked about extending the meaning of language by helping children to elaborate on answers in order to practice making the meaning complex and to put into words the thoughts and logic about the lessons in school. Blank and her colleagues (1978) had a similar notion when they tried to categorize the level of talk that teachers and students used in asking and answering questions. They tried to indicate different levels of talk and to get teachers to monitor their levels of talk with their students of differing ability levels. These attempts to help teachers individualize instruction through their levels of complexity of language is rare in teacher training institutions. The teachers we interviewed had not been trained to monitor their own talk and appeared to have very limited exposure to cultural and ethnic differences that might suggest certain kinds of teacher strategies with children from different backgrounds.

Tizard and Hughes (1984) described the language use of middle- and working-class girls at home and at school in England. The middle-class girls showed continuity between home and school, with their language use similar in each environment. On the other hand, the working-class girls had a difficult time verbally interacting effectively with the teachers at school compared to their ease with verbal interaction in the home.

Our study paralleled this British study (Tizard & Hughes, 1984) in the sense that the Abecedarian children used complex and sophisticated language in their neighborhood but this was not evident in the small ability groups in school. It was possible that by setting up a specific situation for the teacher it might have shown how skilled many of the children actually were, as well as demonstrating teacher effectiveness or non-effectiveness when children did not understand something about new information. We were hoping that the teachers might show us some of the creative teacher strategies that were so eloquently described in *Ways with words* (Heath, 1983) even if they did not use these strategies particularly effectively in the small group situations.

Tutorial Setup

At the beginning of the school year, teachers were told that we were interested in children's learning in a one-to-one situation. We informed the teachers that this situation would be scheduled after they had had time to assess the children's strengths and weaknesses. All sessions in kindergarten and second grade were conducted during the winter months after the New Year. A time was arranged at the convenience of each teacher when she could spend 15 minutes or so alone with both the Abecedarian and the Mainstream child in her classroom. This time was usually during recess or at the time when music or art class was held.

Just before each tutorial began we gave the teacher a wordless picture book. An index card containing two questions was taped above the picture on each page. The teacher was told that we wanted each child to understand the story line in the wordless picture book and the teacher was to ask the prespecified questions about the story as they turned the pages of the storybook. In this way she would be able to assess whether the child was indeed able to comprehend the story through the pictures. She was also told we wanted the child to understand the story as well as possible so it was important for her to follow up on answers that were not adequate in order to help the child get the right answer. She was asked to follow up on any incorrect responses by the child to the questions because these responses would hinder the child's full comprehension of the story line.

The teacher chose the place where the tutorial would be held. Both kindergarten and second grade teachers chose similar settings. Sixty-seven percent of the kindergarten teachers and 70 percent of the second grade teachers chose to go through the storybook at a table or desk in the classroom. Only 12 percent of the kindergarten teachers and 8 percent of the second grade teachers chose to sit on the floor in the classroom. The other teachers chose to use a quiet hallway or other room that contained a table.

At the designated time children and teachers willingly participated. We had only one teacher who refused to do the task with a child. In kindergarten and second grade we asked teachers to ask questions posed by the pictures in a wordless picture book by Mercer Mayer. The kindergarten book was *A Boy, a Dog, and a Frog* and the second grade book was *The Great Cat Chase*. We chose wordless picture books so that the child's oral comprehension of the story was not a factor in their performance, and it also alleviated the large individual differences among teachers in their expressive reading to young children.

On each page of the wordless picture book there were two questions. In all there were 30 questions in kindergarten and 32 questions in second grade. The questions were devised to represent a wide range in complexity, from easy-to-answer concrete questions where the answers were clearly depicted by one of the pictures (generally *who*, *what*, or *where* questions) to abstract questions that required the integration of knowledge about the story as well as the motivations and feelings of the characters (generally *how*, *why*, and *when* questions). From pilot testing, we felt that nearly half the questions would pose problems for the children.

When the teacher was first presented with the book, she was asked to run through it to make sure she understood the story and the questions we wanted her to ask the child. The following instructions were read to her after she had examined the book.

We want you to look at this storybook with _____.
We would like you to ask him/her the questions on each page that assess whether _____ understands the story.
If _____ gives a less than adequate answer, in your mind, please try to follow up on _____'s answer to get her/him to answer correctly. Don't let _____ get on the wrong track or it will make the rest of the story more difficult for _____ to understand.

Both books that we used had interesting story lines that could be understood on several levels. Below is a summary of each story as well as some examples of easy and difficult questions.

A Boy, a Dog, and a Frog

A boy is walking along carrying a net and a bucket and his dog is trotting alongside him. They get to a pond where the boy tries to catch a frog with his net. The boy's attempts are thwarted by a series of humorous strategies gone awry, including catching the dog rather than the frog in the net. Finally the boy gives up and decides to go home. The frog, who had enjoyed being chased, is now all alone in the pond and quite sad. The frog decides to follow the boy and the dog home by following their footprints. The frog finds the boy and his dog in the bath tub and happily decides to join them.

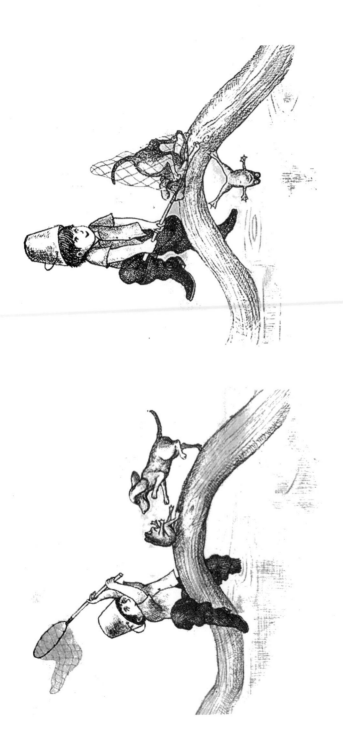

Who did the boy catch? (*Easy*)

Why is the boy smiling? (*Difficult*)

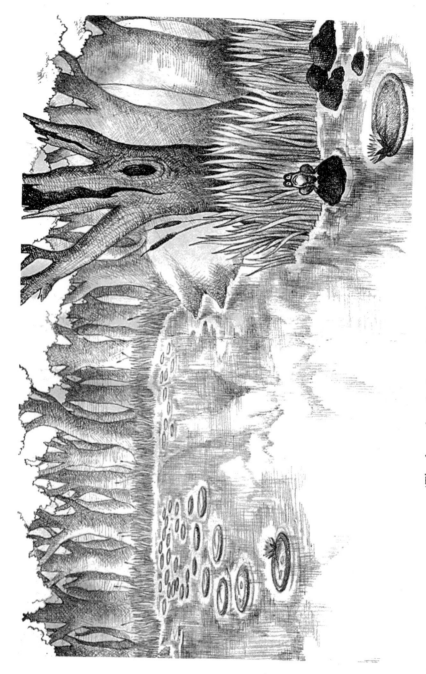

(The frog after the boy and the dog have gone home)
What is the frog thinking? (Difficult)

Why do you think the dog might not like the frog to stay
with the boy always? (*Difficult*)

The Great Cat Chase

A little girl is dressed up like a lady and is pushing her cat in
a baby carriage. There are other children dressed up like adults
also. There is a boy dressed as a policeman and a boy dressed up
as a cowboy. The cat does not want to play the role of the baby
so she jumps out of the carriage and hides. The little girl enlists
the help of the boy-policeman who chases after the cat with the
girl and cowboy trailing behind. After a series of misadventures
where the cat gets the better of the boy-policeman, the policeman
finally catches the cat in a tree, only to have the limb break and
they both fall to the ground. In the end, the girl takes the
frazzled boy-policeman home to give him some lemonade and
the cowboy agrees to be the baby in the carriage while the cat
proudly walks behind.

What is the cat trying to do? (*Easy*)
Why is the boy going along behind? (*Difficult*)

Why does the boy change from being excited to being upset? (*Difficult*)

How are the boy and the cat alike? (*Difficult*)

Children and teachers enjoyed the books and we saw only a few instances of real frustration on the part of either children or teachers. For instance, one teacher threatened to retain the child in kindergarten unless she/he answered the question correctly. After a quick glance at us and an embarrassed "just kidding," she proceeded with the rest of the story.

Children's Skill in Answering Questions

The questions we had devised for the teacher to ask proved quite difficult for all children. For both the Abecedarian and the Mainstream children the percentage of correct responses was below 50 percent. This meant that teachers were forced to follow up on the children's answers to half the questions to help them eventually get the correct answers. Although it might seem that the Mainstream children should have answered more of the questions correctly, there were no differences among the groups on the ability to do so. In kindergarten both groups of children answered about 40 percent of the questions correctly; in second grade they answered about 45 percent of the questions correctly on the first try (see figure 6.1).

Children's Errors in Answering Questions

Although there were no differences between the groups on the number of correct responses, there was some evidence from other sources that the Abecedarian children might have been making different kinds of errors than the Mainstream children; if this was true, teachers might have a harder time responding effectively to the errors of the Abecedarian children.

In order to examine the errors more systematically, we used a modified system to the one proposed by Blank, Rose, and Berlin (1978). This system examined errors that were difficult or easy for teachers to remediate effectively. We classified errors into three major categories: *relevant answer errors, irrelevant answer errors,* and *no response errors.*

Relevant answer errors might be classified as a good kind of

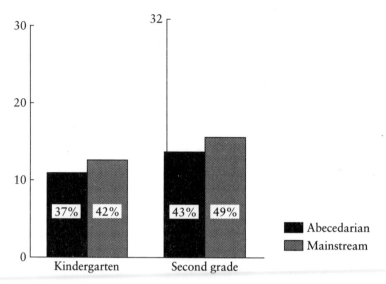

Figure 6.1 Mean Number of Correct Answers, by Group

error because of its closeness to the correct answer. This kind of response was often one that was too general or not complete enough to judge its correctness. For instance, in the kindergarten story *A Boy, a Dog, and a Frog*, the boy has caught the dog by mistake in his net although he thinks he has caught the frog. The question that the teacher asks is, "Why is the boy smiling?" The *correct answer* would be something like "He thinks he caught the frog but he didn't, he caught the dog." However, answers such as "He caught the dog," which is really a description of the picture rather than an answer to the question, or "Uh oh the boy goofed" are not quite right. Both of these answers are related to the correct answer and could be considered *relevant answer errors*. It has been found that teachers are quite good at helping children who make this kind of error get the right answer.

A kind of mistake that appears to be more difficult for teachers to deal with are *irrelevant answer errors*. These answers are often category mistakes that are simply impossible answers to the type of question. The child who makes this kind of error may have completely misunderstood what was required from the form of the question. Thus the child may have given an *irrelevant answer* by saying "tomorrow" (or other response) or "over there" (a placement response) to the question "Why is the boy smiling?" The child who gave an irrelevant answer may not have understood that a "why" question required a causal explanation of some type. These kinds of irrelevant answers were what Blank considered "unteachable" because teachers appeared stymied by such responses and did not have good strategies for getting the child back on track.

The last kind of error was a *no response error*. This happened when a child was either reluctant to answer the question at all or when he/she said something like, "I don't know." This kind of response gave a clear message to the teacher that the child needed some help in understanding how to get the right answer.

When we examined these three kinds of errors across the groups we found a very significant difference between our Mainstream and Abecedarian children on two of the three error types. These differences, depicted in figure 6.2, display the proportion of different types of errors by group and grade.

There were no differences between the groups on relevant answers in kindergarten or second grade, but notice that there was a change from kindergarten to second grade with both groups making proportionately more relevant-type errors. There were significant differences on the irrelevant and no response errors in kindergarten ($p < .01$). Abecedarian children made almost double the proportion of irrelevant answers in comparison to the Mainstream group. In addition, the Mainstream children made double the proportion of no response errors. By second grade the differences were not as dramatic but the Abecedarian children were still making proportionately more irrelevant answer errors in comparison to the Mainstream group.

The reasons for these differences between the Mainstream and the Abecedarian children were probably many but were most surely rooted in the cultural lives of the children. In the observations we made in the neighborhood, the Black children played with language, created their own stories, and rarely were heard answering questions about something unless the answer was unknown by the person who asked the question.

This is clearly not the case in school or in more mainstream

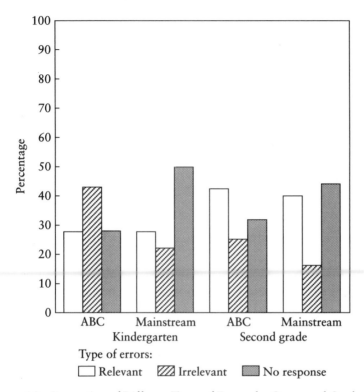

Figure 6.2 Proportion of Different Types of Errors, by Group and Grade

families. When you think about the way in which mainstream adults question children about stories, it is more like a pseudo-test than real questioning. When a story is read by an adult to a child in school and at home in mainstream households, the questions asked by the adults are really rhetorical, because the adult knows the answer to the question. Question-asking is only a pedagogical device to determine whether the child understands the story. The adult is not trying to gain new information about the story, except in rare cases when a more discursive question might be asked.

Certainly in this story task that we presented to the teacher, she knew the answers to the questions and she was trying to get the child to give the right answer. Our Mainstream children probably interpreted this task quite correctly and when they did not know the answer to the question they were silent or said they did not know. On the other hand, the Abecedarian children may have seen the task quite differently and tried to engage the adult in dialogue. These children appeared not to be as concerned about the right answer but more concerned with keeping the dialogue going. They may also have been less aware that the teacher actually knew the right answer since in their home environment pseudo-questions were rarely asked. All the children made many errors but since the two groups of children were making different kinds of errors, we were especially interested in understanding how teachers responded to these different kinds of errors.

Teacher Styles in Response to Child Errors

The differences in error types made by the two groups were interesting but the most critical aspect of the analysis was how the teachers responded to these varying answers by children. We wanted to understand the strategies that teachers used to help the children obtain the right answers to the questions.

We examined teacher responses to answers by dividing responses into five categories. These included an *acknowledgment* or acceptance of the answer. This was sometimes done in the form of praise but often just an "OK" was given. Teachers could also *ignore* a response by merely going on to the next question after the child's answer. Both an *acknowledgment* and an *ignore* were terminal responses in that the teacher went on to the next question after either of these responses. If a teacher believed that the answer was not quite right she could *prod* the child to try again, while providing no additional clues to the answer. The most desirable response to an inadequate answer was for the teacher to *restructure* the question to make it easier for the child to answer or by adding clues that would lead the child more easily to answer the question. We were particularly interested in when and how teachers did this. The final way teachers could respond to answers was to *complicate* the original question, that is, making the original question more difficult by asking it in a more abstract way or by complicating the grammar of the question. In addition, teachers could complicate the original questions by making irrelevant additions that led the child away from the original intent of the question. Table 6.1 summarizes these teacher strategies and gives examples of each.

Teacher Strategies for Correct Responses

Although we expected that teachers would acknowledge correct responses most of the time, that expectation was not borne out by the data. For all groups, teachers acknowledged correct responses less than half the time and they ignored correct responses about 40 percent of the time. Interestingly, teachers asked children to say more about the correct response in about 20 percent of the cases. This included prodding them about 10 percent of the time, restructuring about 5 percent of the time, and actually making the question more complicated more than 5 percent of the time. Figure 6.3 shows the proportion of different kinds of strategies used by teachers in response to correct answers. There were no differences by group, and teachers responded to kindergarten and second grade children similarly.

Teacher Strategies for Relevant Answer Errors

When children gave an incorrect answer, but one that was *relevant* to the answer, teachers used a different pattern of strategies. In this case they accepted the answer by *acknowledging* it almost 30 percent of the time at both kindergarten and second grade and for both groups of children. Teachers in kindergarten *ignored* this type of response half as often as teachers in second grade (15 percent versus 35 percent). Overall, teachers in kindergarten, in comparison to second grade teachers, seemed to be more active in trying to get the child to answer the question. Although there were no group differences at either grade level, it was interesting that teachers accepted these relevant answer errors by either acknowledging or ignoring them 45 percent of the time in kindergarten and 65 percent of the time in second grade.

Kindergarten teachers both *prodded* the child more and *restructured* the questions more often than second grade teachers.

Table 6.1   Teacher Strategies

1. *Acknowledge*	Teacher either reinforces child for response or by verbalization accepts the response. All acknowledge strategies are terminal responses by the teacher and the next question is asked. Example: "Good," "OK."
2. *Ignore*	Ignore responses are those accepted by the teacher but not acknowledged. Teacher goes on to the next question after child answers. She gives no verbal acknowledgment.
3. *Prod*	Teacher repeats question or indicates that the child can answer the question correctly. No new or restructured information is added. Example: "Think, I know you can answer this one." "Let me read the question to you again."
4. *Restructure*	Teacher asks the question in another way by adding new information, making it simpler, breaking it into parts, or capitalizing on previous and shared knowledge. Example: "Remember, the frog likes the boy. How could the frog make himself happier?" "If you were the frog, what would you do?"
5. *Complicate*	Teacher asks the question in another way which makes the question conceptually and syntactically more difficult or changes the question to lead the child away from the correct answer. Example: "How might the frog, if he wanted, make it so that he might be happier when he isn't now?" "You know the frog is on a lily pad and pad rhymes with tad and bad. What else does it rhyme with?"

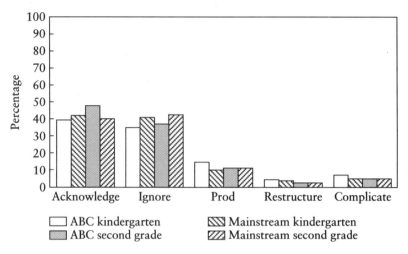

Figure 6.3 Teacher Strategies for Correct Responses, by Group and Grade

It may be the case that at second grade, teachers were more likely to think that the children knew more than they were saying and thus accepted slightly less adequate answers. On the other hand, it may also have been the case that kindergarten teachers were more oriented toward the oral language skills in children and thus were more sensitive to the children's level of understanding and communicative skill. In any case, teachers followed up on these answers only about half the time, even when they were explicitly directed to make sure the child could answer correctly. Figure 6.4 reveals this pattern of differences in responses to relevant answer errors by group and grade.

Teacher Strategies for Irrelevant Answer Errors

Irrelevant answer errors, that have been termed category mistakes or "unteachable responses," were of particular interest since these were made twice as often by the Abecedarian children in comparison to the Mainstream children. Teachers clearly saw this error as more serious than the *relevant answer error*. They accepted this type of response only about 15 percent of the time in kindergarten and 20 percent by second grade. In kindergarten they almost never ignored this kind of error but

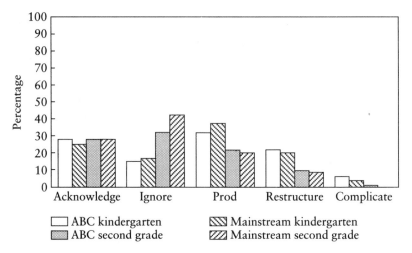

Figure 6.4 Teacher Strategies for Relevant Answer Errors, by Group and Grade

by second grade teachers ignored this error nearly 20 percent of the time. Even though the teachers reacted differently to irrelevant answer errors compared to relevant answer errors, it was surprising to us that this clearly incorrect answer was accepted as an adequate response (*acknowledge* or *ignore*) 20 percent of the time in kindergarten and 40 percent of the time in second grade, especially since these answers are impossible answers to the question.

As in the data from relevant answer errors, teachers in kindergarten were more likely than teachers in second grade to try a strategy to get the child to respond correctly. Generally, teachers in kindergarten tried to *prod* the children into making the correct response about 40 percent of the time. However, children were prodded only about 25 percent of the time in second grade. About 30 to 40 percent of the time, teachers tried to *restructure* the question. This higher rate of restructuring in comparison to that for correct responses and relevant answer errors reflected the teachers' awareness that the child needed help in answering the question. In addition, kindergarten teachers actually made the question more difficult in 10 percent of the cases, probably in a failed effort to try to restructure

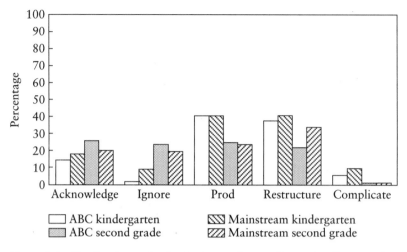

Figure 6.5   Teacher Strategies for Irrelevant Answer Errors, by Group and Grade

the question for the child. Figure 6.5 shows this different pattern of responding by the teacher to irrelevant answer errors. Note that there were no real group differences, except a trend at second grade for the teachers to restructure the questions more often for the Mainstream children in comparison to the Abecedarian children.

Thus, although the teachers clearly responded differently to this kind of error, they used effective strategies less than half the time. Since the Abecedarian children made so many of these kinds of errors, this would result in less effective instruction for them in comparison to the Mainstream children.

Teacher Strategies for No Response Answer Errors

The teacher strategies for the *no response* kind of error were quite remarkable. Although we had expected that teachers would respond with good strategies we did not expect that this kind of response would elicit the best behavior from the teachers. Teachers accepted this response at both grade levels less than 10 percent of the time. Thus, this kind of response, in comparison

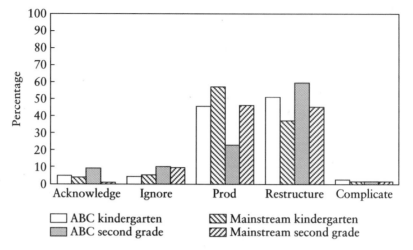

Figure 6.6 Teacher Strategies for No Response Errors, by Group and Grade

to the *irrelevant response*, was much more effective in getting teachers to help children get the right answer. In fact, teachers either prodded or restructured the question 90 percent of the time in comparison to about 60 percent of the time for an irrelevant answer error. In addition, teachers almost never complicated the question. Although there were no striking grade differences, there was a tendency for second grade teachers to prod the Mainstream children and to restructure more for the Abecedarian children. Figure 6.6 shows the pattern of responding.

Implications for Student Learning

These results were somewhat discouraging with regard to our Abecedarian children. Even though they made the same number of correct responses and relevant responses as the Mainstream children (quite an amazing feat given the disparity in resources for the families), the Abecedarian children tended to give irrelevant responses when they did not know the answer to a question while the Mainstream children more often gave no response or said "I don't know." In itself these differences might not really be important except for the fact that teachers responded very differently to these two types of errors. Teachers used much more effective strategies to help children when they gave a no response error: In fact, 90 percent of the time they used strategies to help the child get the right answer. This was not the case for the Abecedarian children who made more irrelevant answer errors. As Blank (1975) had predicted, these "unteachable" responses produced many more ineffective strategies by the teachers. Teachers accepted these irrelevant responses as adequate 20 percent of the time in kindergarten and nearly 50 percent in second grade. Thus they appeared to be stymied by the children's answers since they had the strategies available to remediate the situation but were not able to use them in response to the irrelevant answer error.

This was, of course, only one situation and certainly did not represent all teacher–pupil interactions. However, we believe it was a good and subtle example of how cultural differences among children led to less effective teaching in the classroom. Even good teachers appeared to be unaware of their differential treatment and different effective styles with children. These group differences in teaching style toward the children seemed all the more astonishing because the teachers knew we were watching them and were clearly trying to demonstrate their best practices.

Summary

As part of trying to understand how teachers conveyed new information to children, we devised a bookreading task for teacher and child. In this task teachers were given prespecified questions to ask the children about a wordless picture book. Many of the questions required abstract thinking and problem solving. When children did not answer correctly, which happened over 50 percent of the time, the teachers were asked to follow up on the children's answers to help them get the correct answer. In this way we were able to examine the kinds of errors that children made in answering the questions as well as the strategies that teachers employed to help the children obtain the correct answer.

The results indicated that both the Mainstream and Abecedarian children answered correctly less than 50 percent of the time, but there were striking differences in the kinds of errors that the children made. The Abecedarian children made more *irrelevant answer errors*. These answers were not possible answers to the question type: for instance, answering a "when" question that required a temporal answer with placement words like "over there". The Mainstream children were much more likely to be silent or say "I don't know" when they could not answer a question. We called this error a *no response error*.

These differences were all the more interesting because of the teachers' responses to the different types of errors. Teachers used their best follow-up strategies to help children when the children used a no response error. These strategies included rephrasing the question to make it easier or breaking it into several subquestions. The teachers' worst strategies occurred when the children used irrelevant answer errors, often called unteachable errors. Teachers often ignored these errors or merely asked the question again without modification.

The combination of the children's errors and the teachers' responses to them resulted in poorer feedback to the Abecedarian children since they were the ones who used many irrelevant answer errors. This was particularly interesting since there were no differences between the groups on the number of correct answers given. This may be one type of example of a cultural difference between the groups that led to less effective teaching in mainstream schools for African American children.

7

The Effects of the Intervention on School-Related Skills

It is not possible or appropriate to identify and measure the effects of a single or even several independent variables on intermediate and dependent variables in the complex multivariate system a school program represents. Indeed, such an approach can be analogous to measuring the effects of waving a hand fan at a feather in a wind tunnel. Intervention methods limited to single or several, albeit important, variables in schools are of limited value because of greater importance of variable interaction and change in and out of school on an ongoing basis. Also, variables such as attitudes, morale, and emotions such as hope are extremely difficult to quantify or even describe, but are known to affect school performance.

Comer, 1985, p. 159

The goal of this study has been to describe the transition to school by examining children's experiences at school and at home during the early school years. At the same time there were others connected with the Abecedarian project who were collecting data on academic achievement and other outcome measures that indicated whether children in the intervention group had acquired the skills needed to do well in public school.

These data include periodic individualized testing of IQ and achievement, retrieval of school records, and semi-structured, non-standardized testing of language use.

The results from these more traditional outcome measures of school success have been generally published in journal articles and chapters in books and will be summarized in this chapter as a way to describe more fully how the children fared academically in the school environment. These data were collected at the beginning of kindergarten (age 5), at the end of the third year of school (age 8), and again after seven years in school (age 12).

Intellectual Ability

Improving the intellectual ability of the preschool intervention children was a major goal of the Abecedarian intervention program. The children were tested often during the preschool and school-age years. Previous intervention studies had shown a dramatic increase in IQ due to early intervention and then a diminution in the effect after children entered public school (Lazar et al., 1982; Farran, 1990). The children in our study who had received early daycare intervention were significantly better prepared than the non-intervention group throughout the preschool years. As the children entered school the preschool intervention group maintained their advantage over the preschool non-intervention children through age 12 as detailed by Campbell and Ramey (1994; see figure 7.1). Thus this is one of the few intervention programs that showed the stability of a difference in IQ between the intervention and the non-intervention groups over the early school years. The school-age intervention had no significant effect on IQ.

What is interesting to notice about the pattern of differences in the IQ graph is that both Abecedarian groups began a slight decline in performance upon entering school. Thus for both groups of Abecedarian children the school experience was not one that increased the children's abilities relative to other children, at least as measured by standardized intelligence tests. This was especially evident on the verbal portion of the IQ

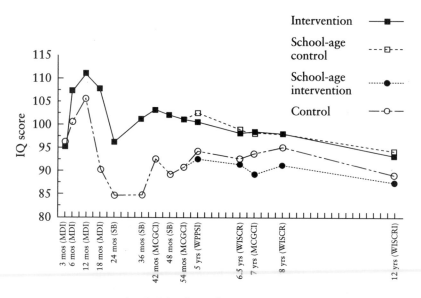

Figure 7.1 Effects of Early Intervention on Intellectual and Academic Achievement: A Follow-up Study of Children from Low-income Families (from Campbell & Ramey, 1994)

tests for the preschool intervention groups. They began school with a verbal IQ above 100 at age 5 but by age 12 they had lost about 4 to 5 IQ points (see Ramey & Campbell, 1991 and Campbell & Ramey, 1994).

Ramey and Campbell (1991) also reported that the preschool intervention prevented children from being classified as mildly mentally retarded (IQ < 70) and from being classified as having a borderline IQ (IQ = 70–85). Again there did not seem to be any effect of the school-age intervention on performance.

Achievement

The achievement of the children was also monitored carefully by administration of the Woodcock–Johnson individualized achievement tests at age 8 and age 12. Although, as with the IQ results, the preschool intervention group continued to outscore the preschool non-intervention group, both groups tended to decline from age 8 to age 12. For instance, according to Ramey and Campbell (1991) the preschool intervention group was close to the 40th percentile in reading and the 45th in math at age 8. The non-intervention group was at about the 20th percentile in reading and the 35th in math. This was clearly an important difference between the groups. By age 12 both groups had declined, especially the preschool intervention group. They dropped about 10 percentile points in reading and about 15 percentile points in math.

Again it was impressive that the preschool intervention had a significant effect on performance but it appeared that the public school experience for both groups of children was not helping to maintain their standing relative to other children the same age. Our findings about the ways in which instruction was delivered to these children in lower ability groups suggest that, although the teachers believed this was the best way to deliver instruction, it did not appear to be aiding the children in performance on standardized achievement and IQ tests. Our classroom observations in ability groups, indicating that less complex material was delivered to most of the Abecedarian children, might help to explain the overall decline in IQ and achievement for both Abecedarian groups.

School records on grade retention (repeating a grade) and the use of special services for academic or behavioral difficulties were difficult to compare over the years but it did appear that there was a trend for less grade retention for the preschool intervention group (Ramey & Campbell, 1991). Even so, over one third of this group had been retained a grade by age 12 while over half of the preschool non-intervention group had been retained. This is in contrast to the comparison group of children in the same classroom, with only 9 percent being retained through age 12. A more complicated picture of the use of special educational services was found, but overall we can say that both groups of Abecedarian children were receiving many more services than the Mainstream children.

Teachers were asked to rate the children on measures of verbal intelligence, considerateness, and extraversion. As with our other public school classroom measures, the teachers did not differentiate between the two Abecedarian groups; both the preschool intervention and non-intervention groups were rated similarly.

Unfortunately, we did not interview teachers with respect to why children were retained or why they were referred for special education services. These data would have been an invaluable contribution in helping to explain both the standardized test data and our observations and tutorials in the classrooms. In summary, many of the Abecedarian children were struggling academically through the school experience. The preschool intervention was a mild buffer against public school experience. Both groups in comparison to children of the same age were generally doing more poorly by age 12 than when they entered the public school.

School-like Language Skills

Another area that was repeatedly assessed for these children was that of language. Because many IQ tests contain verbal portions that tap more traditional language skill, additional measures were added to tap the processes by which children might acquire more fully developed use of language, especially in interaction with others. In addition, at school age children's narrative abilities were assessed, given that narrative skills have been linked to better language use and reading in school (Feagans & Fendt, 1991; Feagans & Short, 1984; Snow et al., 1991; Wells, 1985).

Preschool Language Use

Two studies in the preschool years found an advantage for the preschool intervention children in their use of language. Farran and Haskins (1980) reported that children in the preschool intervention in the toddler years made more initiations with their mothers than the non-intervention group in a laboratory mother–child interaction session. Gordon (1984) found that by age 4 the preschool intervention group was more appropriately responsive to adult initiations in comparison to the non-intervention children in a structured language task.

Language Use in Narratives

The skill of understanding and paraphrasing narratives is clearly a task needed in school since much of the information exchange during the early elementary school years is often in the form of oral exchange about events or instructional lessons. The narrative task described here has been shown to relate well to other measures of school achievement, especially with children at risk for school failure. This task predicted reading achievement better than IQ for a group of elementary school learning-disabled children (Feagans & Short, 1984). Feagans and Appelbaum (1986) used cluster analysis on a group of learning-disabled children that resulted in six subgroups of children who had different patterns of language skills. The subgroup who performed the best on the measures from this narrative task, relative to their performance on more traditional measures of language, also performed better than any of the other subgroups on a reading achievement test three years later. Thus, there is reason to believe that the skills represented in this task are important ones for school success, especially in reading.

The narrative task was given to all children in the fall and spring of kindergarten. The narratives were read to the children, who were asked to demonstrate nonverbally the understanding of the narrative and to then retell the narrative to the adult. Children were presented with an attractive wooden replica of a grocery store. The store contained moveable items on the shelves, a grocery cart, a checkout counter with a clerk, other items commonly found in a grocery store, and boy or girl dolls. Children were asked to listen to a short vignette about the grocery store and then to act out the vignette with the props in the store. If the child did not act out the vignette correctly the story was read again until perfect comprehension was achieved. The grocery store was then covered up and the child was asked to paraphrase the vignette in their own words. At the end the children were asked a series of questions about the vignettes: There were three concrete questions (who, what, where) and three abstract questions (how, why, when).

Children were read three kinds of vignettes, two of each type. Script vignettes were short stories that contained a sequence of events familiar to the child and logically ordered. An example of one story is: "John went into the store. He got a cake for his mother's birthday party. At the checkout counter he paid the clerk. At the end he ran home." The order of events in this vignette is constrained by a real world experience of going to the grocery store. Nonscript vignettes were stories which were not constrained by real world experience but were arbitrarily arranged by the storyteller. The content of the story was familiar to children but not the order of events. An example is: "Mary put bananas in her grocery cart. Then she got some cake. With two hands she put some flour in her cart. It was heavy. Last, Mary pushed the cart to the soup shelf." Knowledge of how to go to the grocery store would not help children remember the events of this vignette in the correct sequence. Temporal vignettes were stories which contained temporal connectives that altered the order of events so that they were counter to the order of mention in the story. An example is: "Before John tripped over the apple on the floor, he had put some cake into his cart. John and the cart fell flat on the floor. John got up quickly and laughed."

Complete details about the task and the results can be found in a series of articles (Feagans & Farran, 1981; Feagans & Farran, 1994; Feagans, Fendt, & Farran, 1995; Feagans & Fendt, 1991). As was true with almost all of the outcome measures in elementary school, the school-age intervention did not show effects on performance, but the preschool intervention did. Overall, we found that the major differences between the preschool intervention and non-intervention groups at kindergarten entry were related to the performance of paraphrasing the story and answering questions about it (Feagans & Farran, 1994; Feagans & Fendt, 1991).

As the children entered kindergarten, the intervention group performed better on this narrative task than the nonintervention group. They were particularly better at including more critical elements in the paraphrase of the vignettes and they used fewer vague references to people and events. By the spring of kindergarten there were few differences between the two Abecedarian groups of children while the Mainstream group performed much better than either of the other two groups of children. Interestingly, the reason for this large gap may have been the better storytelling ability of the Abecedarian children. When we analyzed the paraphrases of the stories, we found that the Abecedarian children, and especially the non-intervention children, tended to add and embellish the vignettes when asked to paraphrase. By doing so they frequently ended up creating a different, but often more interesting, vignette. For instance, one little boy, in paraphrasing the story about John buying a cake for his mother's birthday, proceeded to elaborate on other items he would buy for the birthday party, including hot dogs and potato chips. Even after a reminder that he was to only retell the vignette we had told to him, he created an elaborate story about how he would surprise his mother by inviting many of their relatives and friends. Although these embellishments to the stories often made the paraphrases interesting, this strategy led most of the children to exclude many of the original elements of the vignette (Feagans & Farran, 1981, Feagans, Fendt, & Farran, 1995).

The question-answering task also revealed that the intervention children were doing better at school entry in comparison to the non-intervention children (Feagans & Fendt, 1991). The intervention group answered more questions correctly than the non-intervention group, and indeed answered as well as the Mainstream group of children. As with the results from the teacher–child tutorial, we also found differences on the kinds of errors children were making on the question-answering task. Results suggested that the non-intervention children at school entry made more of the irrelevant response errors. These "unteachable response errors" are the ones that created poor feedback from teachers in the tutorial sessions described in chapter 6 (see figure 6.5). This kind of error was also related to poorer outcomes on IQ and achievement tests in kindergarten. Table 7.1 correlates the question variables with three measures in school: the Weschler Primary Preschool Scales of Intelligence (WPPSI), the Peabody Individualized Achievement Test (PIAT), and the teacher ratings of children's language use (ALI). The use of the irrelevant answer error is especially negatively related to all the IQ, academic, and language use ratings, indicating that use of this error strategy predicted poor school outcomes.

Table 7.1 Correlations of Question Variables with Developmental Markers of School Success

	Non-Intervention			Intervention			Mainstream		
	WPPSI	*PIAT*	*ALI*	*WPPSI*	*PIAT*	*ALI*	*WPPSI*	*PIAT*	*ALI*
Who % correct	.50***	.40**	.37**	.32**	.34*	.35*	.40***	.25	.12
Where % correct	.30*	.22	.14	-.01	-.01	.21	.33*	.34**	.12
When % correct	.56****	.43**	.43**	.25	.18	.22	.29*	.43**	.21
Why % correct	.48***	.50***	.29	.06	.08	.00	.28*	.07	.18
Relevant Answer errors	-.18	.23	.07	.07	.03	-.14	-.25*	-.36**	-.28*
Irrelevant Answer errors	-.48***	-.37*	-.50***	-.38**	-.38**	-.18	-.32**	-.25	-.10
No Response errors	-.27	-.23	.22	-.07	-.15	.13	.02	.11	.05

Note: Because of the high proportion of correct answers to the *what* question type and the low proportion of correct responses to the *how* question type, correlations could not be interpreted.

*p < .05.   **p < .01.   ***p < .001.

The differences between the intervention and the non-intervention group on question answering were not significant in the spring of kindergarten. By that time both groups of Abecedarian children were making more "unteachable errors" compared to the Mainstream group of children. Again, it appeared that the gap between the Mainstream group and the two Abecedarian groups was beginning to grow, even by the end of kindergarten.

Teacher Ratings of Language Use

A questionnaire was developed for use by the teacher that tapped the kinds of skills that were being assessed by the narrative task as well as a few ancillary language skills. The Adaptive Language Inventory (ALI; Feagans & Farran, 1982; Feagans, Fendt, & Farran, 1995) is a teacher rating scale that contains 18 items comprising six subscales. The teacher is asked to rate the child for each item on a four-point scale from "not at all like" to "very much." Four of the six subscales tap the use of language that is considered important for performing well on discourse and narrative material in the classroom. These included *comprehension* of stories and instructions; *production* measured the ability to orally relate narrative information in the classroom as well as answer questions about verbal information; *rephrase* included the ability to recast information which had initially not been understood by others; and *listening* tapped whether the child could sustain attention to discourse and narrative material in the classroom. The last two subscales, *spontaneity* (how quickly and easily the child initiated verbal interaction in the classroom) and *fluency* (how clearly and intelligibly the child spoke), did not appear as important. The teachers were asked to complete the ALI for each child in our study in the spring of the first three years of school. Figure 7.2 shows the results over the three years for the three scales most related to reading achievement (Feagans, Fendt, & Farran, 1995).

Although the Mainstream children were consistently rated better than the Abecedarian groups over the three years, the preschool intervention children were rated better than the

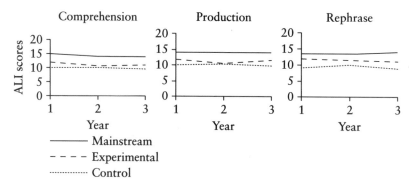

Figure 7.2 Teacher Ratings of Language Over the First Three Years of School

preschool non-intervention children over the same time period. This was particularly true for the *production* and *rephrase* scales. At least the teachers were perceiving a difference in the use of language with respect to the preschool intervention and this effect persisted over three years in school. Teachers did have knowledge of which children received the school-age intervention but not of who had received preschool intervention, so the results are even more important since there were no school-age intervention effects. Although teachers saw the preschool intervention children as more linguistically competent this did not compel them to place these children in higher ability groups or treat them differently in the classroom, as measured by our observations in the classroom.

Summary

There seems to be no doubt that the children who received preschool intervention fared better overall than the non-intervention group with respect to IQ, achievement, and some language use measures as they made the transition to school. This is a testament to the effectiveness of good early intervention. On the other hand, the school-age intervention did not seem to have a large impact on any of the outcome measures.

As both Abecedarian preschool groups progressed through

elementary school they were declining relative to the Mainstream group and to the standardization sample in terms of IQ and achievement. These declines may have been a result of the diminishing effects of the preschool treatment but were more likely to be due to the experience of public schooling since both groups declined in a similar fashion. It is difficult to imagine that either group of Abecedarian children could maintain their abilities when they were placed in lower ability groups that received less complex lessons than those of the Mainstream children.

When they entered school, children's language use was measured through a series of semi-structured narrative tasks and through teacher's ratings of language use in the classroom. All children did well in comprehending the narratives. In the fall of kindergarten, the intervention group outperformed the non-intervention group in paraphrasing the narratives and in answering questions about them. By spring there were few differences between these two groups and both groups performed more poorly than the Mainstream group. Both Abecedarian groups tended to embellish the narratives in their paraphrases instead of telling the story as it had been told to them.

The teachers rated the children's language use in each of the first three years of school. Teachers were asked to evaluate the children's ability to comprehend narratives, their ability to paraphrase and tell stories, and their ability to verbally rephrase information that was not clear. Overall the intervention group was rated better than the non-intervention group over the three years on the three major language use scales. The teachers rated the Mainstream children better than either of the Abecedarian groups.

Overall, the intervention group performed better intellectually, academically, and linguistically than the non-intervention group at the beginning of school. Some of this advantage by the intervention group decreased over the elementary school period, especially in relation to the performance of the Mainstream children. Both the intervention group and the non-intervention group declined somewhat in IQ and achievement over elementary school while the Mainstream children did not show this difference in performance.

8

Success for All Children in School

You are valued in this program because of your academic potential – regardless of your current skill level. You have no more to fear than the next person, and since the work is difficult, success is a credit to your ability, and a setback is a reflection only of the challenge.

Steele, 1992, p. 75

The complex set of factors that contribute to the multiple problems of many poor and minority children can often lead us away from focussing on the strengths of these children and their families that can help us prevent the children's failure to thrive in the school environment. Almost all children, no matter what their background, come to school ready and eager to learn. The Abecedarian children came to school with great hopes for success and had families who valued education and had high aspirations for their children's educational future. Although some of the teachers we encountered saw the strengths that our children brought to school, most saw only the many reasons why the children were not doing as well as others in school. It seemed clear to us that the teachers were the ones not ready when our children entered school. Yet, the failure of most children in school is generally attributed to the poorly prepared student, not to inadequately prepared teachers.

To avoid the perils of school we must first transform the

way schools and teachers think about the large individual differences among children as they enter school, and to subscribe to the quote that introduces this chapter. This means changing the mainstream belief system that has convinced many, and especially our teachers, that poor and minority children do not have the richness of experiences and the skills to benefit from the mainstream education in our schools. Changing this mainstream belief system to convey to all children that they have the potential to learn, and more importantly that attributions of failure to acquire competence should be assigned to us, the adult teachers who are responsible for teaching our children, is a daunting task. It is especially challenging to try to suggest specific strategies that can break the cycle of attributions of incompetence and failure that have characterized adult mainstream beliefs about poor and African American children as these children are forced through the current educational system.

These needed changes in beliefs about child learners are all the more challenging to tackle because the motivations behind the present practices in early intervention programs and public schools have generally been benevolent and the adult participants have believed so fervently in the rightness of their approach to schooling. It would be much easier if the problem could be solved by a new and attractive workbook or a new phonemic approach to reading. These kinds of concrete solutions are always easier to implement and are often suggested at the end of studies like this in an attempt at a local solution to a larger global problem. Unfortunately, no such simple solution is possible. No new curriculum materials will really help. What is needed is a transformation in the underlying philosophy of the educational system that places the onus of responsibility for child failure in school on the educational system and not on the individual child and his/her family or community.

In this chapter I will try to lay out some of the features of this mainstream belief system in Western culture and some strategies that may help the Abecedarian children of the future avoid the perils of school. The focus of change suggested in this book is grounded locally within each school and educational system so that the teachers of the future will dedicate themselves to success for all the children in their home community. At present, the mainstream belief system about poor and minority children is transmitted to the children who themselves develop the belief that failure is always looming for them on the horizon. As one older boy in the Abecedarian community commented to one of our Abecedarian kindergartners, "See, Melvin, you stop likin to go to school when you get there."

How to get Melvin and other non-mainstream children to like school and do well may not be such a difficult task when we, as educators, have the training to use the strengths of our children to assure that they can see success in school as attainable.

Belief Systems and the Macroenvironment

Although our Abecedarian study was a micro study of home, community, and school for one small group of poor African American children, the implications from the study seem to point to the larger Western culture as the cause of the way in which the children viewed the schooling process and of the way they were viewed as learners in the intervention program and at school. The process of schooling that the children in our study were experiencing reflected the values and beliefs of the larger society. These beliefs were embodied not only in the larger educational system but also in the Abecedarian project that adopted a compensatory approach to helping these children in the early years of life. The beliefs were transmitted to the children in the form of benevolent paternalism – that because of their environment at home they needed extra compensatory programs in the preschool years and help when they entered the public school system. There is no doubt that many of the Abecedarian children did not have "mainstream experiences" like nightly bookreading, regular visits to libraries, and other "educational experiences." But the experiences they did have in their home communities were just as rich and complex. These included creative storytelling and rhyming games in concert with other people in the community, both children and adults. These experiences and traditions were not capitalized upon when the children entered public school. Further, there was a sense about all the compensatory programs in preschools and elementary schools that stressed changing the children to "fit the system." The effects of this complex belief system have had broad-ranging influence on the entire schooling of individual poor and minority children, an influence that parallels in some ways the effects of other macrobeliefs and events of the past that have shaped the lives of children in the United States and other Western countries.

We can learn from previous studies of children that events and the interpretation of these events by the larger society can have significant effects on the lives of individual children. Bronfenbrenner (1979) has written much about how this macrosystem of cultural beliefs, policies, and laws influences the lives and development of children. Glen Elder's classic work (1974, 1979; Elder & Rockwell, 1978) examined the effect of the Great Depression on children's development. This macro-event in the United States was experienced in different ways by various families, having both positive and negative effects on the children studied. For instance, Elder found that if the family system had been stable prior to the Depression, the children were able to survive the stress of economic loss. But if the family was not stable before the Depression, then the stress of the father's loss of work and subsequent sense of failure had profound effects on the future of the children in the family, especially the boys. This is a good example of how events in the larger society can have quite direct effects on the family and on the belief systems within the family that get translated into failure beliefs by the child.

Although the Elder study may be one of the best examples of an analysis of the effect of a macro-level system on the beliefs and behaviors of individual children and their families, the Great Depression was a relatively easily identifiable event that helped shape the lives of children at that time. Much less obvious and more insidious forces shape the lives of the children of today. The belief system that discriminates against certain ethnic minorities and children who are misnamed "disadvantaged" has certainly been identified as a problem in this larger macrosystem, but what have not been adequately addressed are the assumptions that underlie the belief system and lead to the larger society's solution to these observed inequities among children. These beliefs need to be explicitly stated and challenged if there is to be change, and these assumptions are often rooted in good intentions that make recognition of them and change more difficult.

The following beliefs need to be changed within the macro-environment of our communities and schools before real change for poor and minority children can occur. The results of our study suggest that four beliefs together created myths in the educational system that were transmitted to the children early on in their school careers. These myths made failure much more inevitable for these non-mainstream children, who eventually came to believe in them. There are two myths about the children's backgrounds: the myth of disadvantage/difference and the myth of family and community dysfunction; and two myths about the children themselves: the myth of poor motivation and the myth of poor ability.

The Myth of Disadvantage/Difference

At the beginning of this book, "disadvantaged" was discussed as it related to poor and minority children. Although this term has generally been redefined with other terms like "difference," it continues in other forms in the preparation of teachers who will eventually try to teach many of the poor children in Western countries.

A book entitled *Schooling disadvantaged children* (Natriello, McDill, & Pallas, 1990) is a good example of the authors' right motives but false beliefs that led them to use the word "disadvantage" with respect to poor and minority children. The authors of this book even review the dispute about using the word "disadvantaged" and yet persist in using it anyway. They say that critics argue there are two reasons not to use this term when talking about poor or ethnically diverse populations. These critics argue that defining a group of children as disadvantaged misdirects the intervention efforts away from the institutions that are responsible for educating children and focusses more on the problems of the children themselves. The onus is placed on the wrong people. Secondly, identification of children as "disadvantaged" can also lead to a self-fulfilling prophecy that can hinder children's learning. That is, the children begin to believe they are disadvantaged and see themselves as not being able to succeed. Both of these arguments are cogent reasons to avoid using the term "disadvantaged."

Even after acknowledging the credibility of the criticism, Natriello et al. (1990) decided to use the word "disadvantaged" but broadened the definition so that disadvantage could occur in three places: the home, the community, and/or the school. This was certainly a better use of the construct but it still allowed the educational institution to blame the victim for failure. For instance, the authors used the following example in their working definition of "disadvantage" that indicted the families and communities they purported to help.

> There are several implications of this definition that deserve special comment. First, families and communities may be viewed as educationally deficient without necessarily being socially deficient. For example, a strong, loving family may simply be unequipped to provide an educationally stimulating environment for its children. This may stem from cultural differences that make experiences in the family incompatible with those in U.S. schools or from economic limitations that leave families without sufficient resources beyond those necessary for survival. (p. 13)

This kind of argument has been just the one that has led many benevolent educators to create a paternalistic system that devalues the experiences of children out of the mainstream. Most families out of this mainstream culture provide very stimulating experiences for their children and have often created valuable learning experiences for them, but these experiences have not always been the ones valued by the mainstream schools. What is needed is to change the attitudes of the educational establishment in order to capitalize on the experiences of children from different backgrounds, without devaluing them.

The term "different background" has been used more recently to describe the experiences of poor and ethnic minorities but the same negative conclusion has been drawn by the educational system, that is, that the children were not prepared or ready to learn when they entered school. Although it has been generally agreed that "different," rather than "disadvantaged," is a more neutral term, both terms imply that children living in poverty will need compensatory programs either in the preschool years or upon entering school and that it is likely that they will not progress through the curriculum at the same speed as more mainstream children (Ogbu, 1982).

These attitudes and beliefs by the educational system are communicated to the children in the classroom through such practices as ability group formation and the segregation within the classroom of those with certain skills. These attitudes about ability to learn are further reinforced by the actual practices that teachers employ. Thus, the Abecedarian children were discriminated against in two rather different ways.

First, no matter what their potential, our Abecedarian children were almost uniformly placed in low-ability groups. This practice reflected the teachers' assumptions that children reared in poverty needed compensatory programs and were unlikely to progress at a rapid rate and to function at the same level as children from more privileged backgrounds. Although all teachers said they believed children could progress to higher ability groups and that placement in lower groups did not mean less complex material was being presented, our data suggest that this was not the case. Teachers were all well prepared and handled the groups well. Yet the complexity of the lessons in the high-ability groups was higher than in the lower ability groups and teachers seemed to be more comfortable and effective with these higher groups.

Second, our Abecedarian children were discriminated against at the teaching level also. Even at the individual level in our contrived tutorial, we found that teachers were less effective in giving feedback to our Abecedarian children – not because the children were less competent but because the children replied in ways that the teachers were not able to deal with effectively. Teachers did not appear to have experience with the kinds of strategies our minority children used when they did not know the answer to a question. Our Abecedarian children often gave the same number of incorrect answers as Mainstream children, but teachers were unable to effectively follow up on the answers of the Abecedarian children to help them get the right answer. On the other hand, the Mainstream children often said nothing or "I don't know" when they did not know the answer to a question. Teachers were much more effective in helping children who responded in this way.

Both of these results from our study show the Abecedarian children to be further at risk for not succeeding in school despite their desire to do so and their level of competence. The very belief that these children were somehow disadvantaged led teachers to attribute to them less ability for their future success in school. The teachers acted upon these beliefs by placing the children in low-ability groups and by being less able to teach them despite their equal competence with their more advantaged peers.

Although the Abecedarian preschool intervention was much more benign than the public school, the myths of disadvantage were clearly evident in this earlier setting also. The "middle-class" way with words was the ultimate goal for the language, cognitive, and social development of the Abecedarian intervention. Chapter 3 revealed these common myths of disadvantage since the project explicitly stated that its goal was to make the Abecedarian children more "middle-class." For instance, the curriculum stressed improving the children's language skills to be more complex, thus more "middle-class" (McGinness, 1982). Yet, our observations indicated that the language skills of the Abecedarian children were as good as or better than those of the Mainstream children. The paternalistic benevolence was delivered with the wrong assumptions. This kind of benevolence communicates to children that their home environments do not serve them well in the schooling process and they do not have the tools necessary to do well unless they change. These beliefs put children in conflict with their home community and also give them a somewhat fatalistic view of their future in school, even if they come with the skills they need.

A number of studies (Alexander & Entwisle, 1988; Steele, 1992) have documented that most African American children come to school with similar skills to other poor children. Yet over the first few years of school, these African American children fall progressively further behind their peers. As Margaret

Donaldson said (1978), these small gaps between children at school entry get wider if they are not soon closed. The myth of disadvantage can help widen these gaps, even with good intentions of remediation and compensatory programs.

The Myth of Family and Community Dysfunction

Closely related to the belief about "disadvantage" are the myriad myths about the families and communities of these children. This study has reported much about the families and communities of the Abecedarian children. Most of them came from single-parent, mother-headed households. This fact, coupled with poverty, can be a negative predictor of school success but within these families are many strengths that can compensate for father absence and lack of economic resources. Unfortunately these "social address" variables (such as single parent, poverty, and social class) are laden with social values that mark children from these types of backgrounds as coming from dysfunctional family environments. Notions like "single parent" and the customary accompanying poverty evoke images of a poor family life for these children. These social address variables do not describe the processes that actually occur in families and these terms have done much to malign an often benign family system that is there to support the child, even with its limited economic resources.

Although some of the Abecedarian families were dysfunctional, and the grinding poverty had affected deeply the home life of the children, most families had great strengths. Most of the children had many family members who cared about them and who clearly valued the children's success in school. As was seen in the interviews conducted with both Mainstream and Abecedarian families, all families highly valued education and saw it as the avenue for the ultimate success of their children. The beliefs about families and communities and even beliefs about what was best for children were similar across both the Mainstream and Abecedarian groups of families. Both groups had even saved money for their children's future college years.

Our sample of children may have been somewhat different from other poor and minority populations due to their residing in a town away from a big city and because of their link to the land in the Southern part of the United States. But many families who do struggle each day with the violence and crime so often prevalent in big cities continue to hope for a better life for their children in school. LaJoe, the mother in *There are no children here* (Kotlowitz, 1991), continued to support her children's success in school despite the unbelievable suffering and societal alienation she had endured over the years. Even in this present study, I think it would have been a surprise to most of the teachers in University Town and Milltown who taught our Abecedarian children that our families had the same high aspirations and values about school as did the Mainstream families.

One area where actual differences existed between the two groups of families was in child-rearing practices. The Abecedarian families almost uniformly used physical punishment for transgressions by children while the Mainstream families used this form of punishment only occasionally. Much has been written in the middle-class research literature about the "evils" of physical punishment of children and the myth has been created that such practice borders on child abuse. No doubt there are families in which physical punishment can lead to abuse, and coupled with poverty and the stress of family life this form of punishment may indeed be dysfunctional, but the judicious use of physical punishment should not be dismissed as merely a "bad" parenting practice without understanding its roots and its effect on the children.

In our interviews with the families, physical punishment was used with forethought in cases of disobedience or cruelty to others. Families believed in the rightness of this discipline approach and even allowed those outside the family who had authority in the community to use physical punishment on their children. This form of punishment had been used within their culture for as long as they knew and had produced good and kind adults. Yet these good effects have often been dismissed by the mainstream research and clinical community without serious consideration or research into its uses.

In another book on the topic of inner-city minority youth, Nightingale (1993) falls into the trap of assigning physical punishment by families as a cause for at least some of the violence and suffering of inner-city children. Again, the victims are blamed. Nightingale certainly made good arguments about the need to decrease the excessive use of violence on children by their parents, but he failed to understand the historical roots of judicious physical punishment in the Black culture that had led to good outcomes for children in the past. In the quote below Nightingale fails to respect the African American values that allow for physical punishment of children.

> The particular enthusiasm for American traditions of forceful child rearing among inner-city parents – and their rejection of "progressive" philosophies – also reflects their own experiences of indignities and powerless feelings brought on by poverty, troubles with employment, and racism. However, for both parents and children, the tradition itself, the respectability of its Christian and mainstream origins, and the official sanction it receives from the law-and-order policies of America's police, courts, and prisons all help to make the forceful child-rearing approach an important source of legitimacy for values of violence in the inner city. Also, the tradition can be used all too often to legitimate parental behavior that leaves children with hurtful and even traumatic memories. (p. 81)

It has been easy for the more mainstream culture to overlook the important role that "good" and carefully constrained physical punishment played in the history of the African American people in the United States. In the families we interviewed they pointed with pride to the leaders of their community who had been reared by the rod. The use of physical punishment in order to produce "good" Christians had been successful in producing non-violent, gentle people. For most of the families, physical punishment was not used in anger or for retribution but as the right way to rear children.

It is important to distinguish between the physical punishment of children used judiciously and consistently for children's moral transgressions, rule breaking, and safety violations and the physical punishment of children used inconsistently and out of frustration by parents and other adults angry with life and transmitting this frustration and anger to their children. The former characterized the parents in our sample, a form of discipline aimed at developing character and moral integrity, while the latter would surely be considered abuse by both the Mainstream and the African American community.

Nightingale (1993) writes in frustration about trying to change the discipline practices of inner-city parents and how the African American parents refused to take the advice and counsel of good-hearted social workers who wanted parents to talk to their children about transgressions and to use non-violent means of discipline whenever possible. Unfortunately, these well-intentioned social workers were unaware of the strong historical tradition of physical punishment that had been successful in producing the best African Americans among them. Without understanding the important cultural significance of physical punishment these social workers were doomed to failure in trying to change the discipline practices used in these families. We may all decry severe physical punishment, but the myth that this practice is always wrong and should never be used devalues again an African American cultural tradition that has worked well in the past. This type of upbringing certainly produced the civil rights workers of the 1960s who decried violence and who were willing to be beaten and jailed for the seeking of equality. It is no wonder that the inner-city African American parents of whom Nightingale spoke only paid lip service to the suggestions of social workers. I am sure that to many minority parents it would seem that the non-violent child-rearing practices of middle-class mainstream America had not served them well as they looked at the violence inflicted upon them from the more mainstream culture, a culture that condemned the use of physical punishment on their children.

This myth of "bad" child-rearing practices has been supported in the schools by the lack of acknowledgment of the legitimacy of physical punishment in certain settings. One of our mothers described an all too typical incident that reflected this conflict in values between the Mainstream and the African American discipline practices. The mother was describing how she had "popped" her child (a quick loud spank on the backside of the child) for talking back to an adult at a Sunday picnic. The child, who was only 8 years old, turned around and threatened the mother by saying, "I'm gonna tell my teacher on you. You'll see, you're not supposed to hit children. You can go to jail." Although this further back talk resulted in another quick "pop," the mother said she was a bit worried about her child saying anything about the incident to a teacher in the Mainstream school, but mostly she was angry that the schools did not support the discipline practices of most of the Abecedarian families. This mother believed the public schools were not strict enough and allowed children to misbehave without adequate punishment. Clearly, the schools may not want to sanction the physical punishment of children but if the schools had been able to recognize the legitimacy of judicious physical punishment they could have helped to prevent the further alienation of the African American families. This negative message from the schools about disciplinary values was yet another way the system devalued the families of the Abecedarian children.

The Myth of Lack of Ability/Skill

The third myth, and the first related directly to the child, is the child's lack of ability or skill. Although the strong version of this myth was laid to rest by the late 1960s, it remains today in a more subtle but often insidious form. Especially within the educational community, educators have been in general agreement that "lack of ability" was a false premise. The remnant left from the response to the "lack of ability" arguments generally acquiesced that these poor and mostly minority children did not have the skills to do well in school and that some form of remediation was needed in order for the children to succeed. This myth has been recently represented by the book *The bell curve* (Herrnstein & Murray, 1994) that suggests that minority children are inevitably intellectually inferior to Caucasians, and that early interventions are generally useless. Even in the most benign of classrooms, the myth of lack of ability can show itself. In one instance one of our children with the highest ability (IQ about 130) was placed in one of the lower ability groups in kindergarten and second grade. She was placed there largely by virtue of her ethnicity and poverty, which were markers for the teachers that she was lacking in some skill or experience.

Even in cases where African Americans have "made it" within the system, they seem to be continually confronted with expectations of failure. In his autobiographical book about growing up African American in the United States, Staples (1994) recalls one of his first academic experiences in graduate school at the University of Chicago. As he talked to a faculty member about one of the classes she was to teach, she said to him, "We have been horrible to the Black people, we have treated them so badly. We have to make it up. It may take you a little longer to get the degree, but you will get it" (p. 26). This benevolent but paternalistic attitude had its impact. Staples' reaction to this statement probably reflects in many ways the thought processes in the minds of our Abecedarian children in their early school years. He wrote about his reaction to the well-intentioned psychology professor:

> I was numb. It seemed Erika [professor] had told me that I was a dull child, to be treated with pity and patience, that I should accept her condolences in advance for the difficulty I would have. The best I could do was nod until I got my senses back.
>
> Back at the hotel, I went over my documents. The transcript said "dean's list, dean's list, dean's list." It said Alpha Chi National Scholarship Honor Society. It said *cum laude* graduate, and I cursed myself for falling six one-hundredths of a percentage point short of *magna cum laude*. I read again the wilted clipping from *The Delaware County Daily Times* – "Brent A. Staples . . . has won a Danforth Fellowship for advanced study for the Ph.D. degree." . . . Nowhere did the story say that I was a foundling who'd gotten into college by accident. (pp. 26, 36)

Steele (1992) analyzed in depth why so many Black students fail in the school system when other poor children who are not Black do not fail at the same high rate. This Black scholar argues that the devaluation of their ability and skill is almost inescapable.

Sooner or later it forces on its victims two painful realizations. The first is that society is preconditioned to see the worst in them. Black students quickly learn that acceptance, if it is to be won at all, will be hard-won. The second is that even if the Black student achieves exoneration in one setting – with the teacher and fellow students in one classroom, or at one level of schooling, for example – this approval will have to be rewon in the next classroom, at the next level of schooling. Of course, individual characteristics that enhance one's value in society – skills, class status, appearance and success – can diminish the racial devaluation one faces. And sometimes the effort to prove oneself fuels achievement. But few from any group could hope to sustain so daunting and everlasting a struggle. Thus, I am afraid, too many Black students are left hopeless and deeply vulnerable in America's classrooms. (p. 74)

The myth of poor ability and skill can be so devastating because it really never seems to be laid to rest. This is one myth that must be actively argued against from the beginning, and it must be made clear to the child that he or she has come to school with the necessary skills to learn if he or she works hard.

The most poignant example of this process was brought home to me when I observed Lena, one of our intervention children, in her kindergarten classroom. Her teacher had instructed all the children to draw a picture about the story she had just read to them. Lena had drawn an abstract drawing in black and white that, in my opinion, was quite creative. As part of the teaching/learning process, this particular teacher had each child hold up their drawing for the whole class, explain its significance, and get feedback from the class in the form of "Yeah!" or "Nay!" Lena was clearly anxious about her performance but at some level she must have felt quite confident since all previous children had received "Yeahs" from their peers. When Lena was asked to show her picture, she was particularly inarticulate and anxious. Her peers booed her. As the tears welled up in her eyes and eventually trickled down her cheeks, the teacher quickly moved on to the next child without so much as a comforting comment to Lena. How could anyone be anything but appalled by such seemingly uncaring behavior?

What must Lena have thought about her competence as an artist and student? Unfortunately all I could do was smile and give her the sign that I thought she had done a fine job, a fairly feeble response to a devastating school experience.

In the data presented in this book the Abecedarian children behaved similarly to the Mainstream children in their ability groups and were able to correctly answer questions posed to them about the picture stories just as often as the Mainstream children. Yet, the treatment of the children in the classroom indicated that the Abecedarian children were considered less skilled. This was manifested in many of the comments the children made about their school experience. Even by the beginning of kindergarten our children were projecting failure for themselves in school. There appeared to be a hopelessness about their future school prospects, even though they wanted to do well.

The Myth of Poor Motivation

This fourth myth is usually directly attributed to the children themselves and is often a result of behaviors by the children that make the educational system attribute to them poor motivation to learn. This perceived lack of motivation is often seen as a reflection of the lack of ambition on the part of the children, that the children do not want to better themselves, that they do not value formal schooling. Nothing could be further from the truth.

Steele (1992) has discussed this persistent mythology about Black Americans and its tragic effects on children's own belief systems during the schooling process. He argues that the mainstream beliefs about Black achievement in school cause what he calls "disidentifying with school." During this process of disidentification, children who come to school ready to learn quickly surmise that their experiences have been devalued by the educational system. The schools have undermined the value of their home community, their experiences at home, their parents' child-rearing strategies, and their own abilities. Just when these children need to see school as a critical setting for the development of self-worth, they realize that for them this is unlikely to happen. The devalued status of their ethnicity and economic circumstances in turn devalues them. The result is children who eventually do not care about school in order to make themselves less vulnerable to the future failure they see in school.

Steele argues that this disidentification can spread quickly in schools and that defectors from it can be ostracized by other Black children. Thus for Black students the pressure to disidentify comes from the already demoralized, as we saw in the conversation with Melvin from our Abecedarian study and also by the beliefs of the mainstream system itself. Steele has described this process in college but it happens at every level of the schooling process.

> She disidentifies with achievement; she changes her self-conception, her outlook and values, so that achievement is no longer so important to her self-esteem. She may continue to feel pressure to stay in school – from her parents, even from the potential advantages of a college degree. But now she is psychologically insulated from her academic life, like a disinterested visitor. Cool, unperturbed. But, like a painkilling drug, disidentification undoes her future as it relieves her vulnerability. (p. 74)

In the Abecedarian study we found the mainstream schools reinforced the devaluation of minority children not only by the placement of children in lower ability groups but also by the way in which teachers and adults responded to the children during interaction with them. We documented how, even at the micro level of individual interactions with children, misattributions of motivation can take place when the teachers are not aware of the children's culture and when they are steeped in their own cultural myths about poor and minority children.

One example of the micro-level myths was the tutorial situation that we presented to teachers and children in which the teachers asked the children a series of questions about a wordless picture book. Teachers more often ignored the category mistakes made by our Abecedarian children and moved on to the next question. These frequent errors were responses not relevant to the question asked. The teachers, in response to these errors, helped the Abecedarian children less often to get the right answer to the question. On the other hand, when children said "I don't know" or were silent, as was characteristic of the Mainstream children, the teacher was quite good at helping them get the right answer.

Why was this the case? In part it was probably due to the fact that teachers did not know how to effectively deal with the kinds of responses that our Abecedarian children gave and so they merely ignored the wrong answer; however, when we asked the teachers why they ignored these irrelevant answers so often and did not help the children get the right answer, their responses also reflected a misattribution about the children's motivation. Some of our teachers said that the children's answers showed that they were not taking the story seriously or had not listened carefully to the question being asked. Yes, the teachers believed that the Abecedarian children more often lacked motivation and were less serious about the task in hand. They did not make these same attributions about the answer "I don't know" that the Mainstream children made more often.

The other more micro way that teachers and other adults made misattributions about motivation related to how the children handled narrative material. We knew from our more structured tasks and from our observations in the neighborhood that storytelling was a valued activity in the Abecedarian communities. But it differed in some important ways from the way Mainstream children told stories. In their home setting the Abecedarian children were encouraged to embellish stories so that if the same story was retold there would be some different elements to make it more interesting, especially if the audience had already heard the story. In the mainstream culture and in school, children were expected to retell stories as accurately as possible without embellishment. In fact, verbatim recall was really encouraged and teachers praised children who could perfectly retell stories that had been read in school. Our Abecedarian children, when asked to retell a story read at school, would embellish and reconstruct it, even after direct instructions to tell the story as it had been told to them (Feagans & Farran, 1981, 1994). But since they had not yet learned the school ways they retold more interesting but more inaccurate versions. The teachers, and even some of us researchers, saw this behavior as defiant or at the least as displaying a lack of motivation for listening to the story in the first place. Thus differences in performance between children from different backgrounds were seen by the mainstream school in terms of "lack of motivation," conspiring in subtle ways to devalue the Abecedarian children.

So How Do We Help These Children Avoid the Perils of School?

The solution to each of the problems posed by the four myths is complex, but the first step is to admit that these four beliefs have permeated Western culture. The mere admission of their reality would help to validate and legitimate the experiences of minority children. But the change that is needed must happen at several different levels of society. There are three major ways in which change can be implemented at a more micro level. These include the development of better administrator/teacher preparation at our colleges and universities that stresses the philosophical and historical underpinnings of mainstream and minority cultures. Second, this means the new involvement of the Black community in the schooling of children. This involvement should not be limited to parents but should include community leaders, mentors, and ministers as well. Third, an emphasis should be placed on mentoring all children. Participatory learning and apprenticeship at one time was a part of all educational systems and has consistently shown its merit for naive learners. We should capitalize on the resurgence of this important teaching/learning strategy.

Teacher Preparation

The National Commission on Children issued its final report in 1991. The recommendations in that report called for a number of changes in our educational system that would especially help children in poverty and those from minority groups. One of the strongest recommendations made was to improve the effectiveness of principals by encouraging the creation of School Based Management systems. James Comer (1992) initiated these kinds of systems in New Haven, Connecticut and they have been effective in creating successful inner-city schools. Parents and teachers participate in what he calls a Governance and Management team that allows parents and teachers to work together on the policies and practices within the school. In addition there is a team of mental health professionals and parents who intervene during crises of individual children as well as trying to create a healthy atmosphere for learning within the school. The parent participation program is very strong and helps the larger community invest heavily in the success of all the children in the school.

This kind of change in the way schools operate depends on the initiative of the principal as well as his or her training and willingness to share the power within his or her school. This kind of training should be institutionalized in universities and colleges so that the more autocratic style is seen as dysfunctional in a pluralistic multicultural society.

Teachers also need to learn from their university training and experience that sharing their time and joint decision-making with parents and community leaders does not diminish their effectiveness in the classrooms. The "back to basics" mandate has often been interpreted by teachers and principals as a call to focus efforts on the details of the curriculum to ensure that standardized test scores for their classroom and school are at the very highest level, without regard for teaching all the children. With the more multicultural approach, and with goals that stress success for all children, there should be more emphasis on teaching strategies that address different cultural backgrounds and a refocus to the enhancement and enjoyment of learning. Standardized test scores would be only one of the many indexes of successful teaching.

Most important of all in teacher education is to be sure future teachers are aware of the false beliefs about poor and minority children that seeps into the teaching practices of even the most well-meaning among our teachers. This requires a careful examination of the content of what is taught and the value judgments implicit in each lesson as well as in the discipline thought to be appropriate. Currently the subtle devaluation of minority beliefs and practices is communicated to the children and, in turn, can have devastating long-term effects on their beliefs about themselves and the success they have in school. Instead of making sure that every child comes to school ready to learn, each teacher needs to be ready to teach every child who comes to school. This message, that places the onus on all of us for the success of children, could have an enormous impact on the way in which teachers approach teaching all children.

This study, like so many others, reveals the disparity in the level of teaching between high- and low-ability groups. Clearly, our teacher education curriculum needs to focus on how to teach effectively in groups that contain children of different abilities and skills. The perpetuation of the ability group system from early elementary school ensures that the Abecedarian children and others like them will never learn or be exposed to the same level of complex thinking and learning. How to change the way teachers group children for instruction is a challenge for the future if we truly want equality in our schools.

Unfortunately, these changes are hard to accomplish without the support of the community and administrators within the school district. Hopefully, national leadership and community pressure can encourage these changes, especially within schools that serve poor and minority children.

Involvement of Parents and Community

The involvement of parents and community is assumed by the changes required of principals and teachers, but parents and community leaders within the poor and minority communities should not wait to find the right principal and teachers. Even though children may be bussed from other parts of the community to elementary school, parents and other caring adults must make the effort to become engaged with the children's schools. This may take the efforts of church leaders, forging alliances with respected adults in the community who are willing to become involved with school administrators, teachers, and individual students.

This kind of effort characterized many Head Start programs that are, unfortunately, still quite separate from the educational establishment in the community. From the beginning, Head Start has been an impressive example of the importance of community and parent involvement (Zigler & Muenchow, 1992). Although the planning committee for Head Start took bold steps to involve parents in the program as consultants and participants with their children, they did not envision that parents would control the program in any major way. The leadership of the Community Action Program (CAP) was the host agency for Head Start and created a new dimension to parent involvement that was even more revolutionary in conception and, for many, even more difficult to accept than the original one. According to CAP, the roots of the problem for poor and minority children lay in racism and classism that resulted in disenfranchisement from the mainstream White culture. From their perspective the children did not have deficits or poor parenting. They saw Head Start as an opportunity to establish an alternative power structure for the Black community that had influence on the educational system of the country and could be a forum for preparing their children for public school.

This new conception of parental involvement met with some resistance in the Head Start movement because parents were seen as having too much power if they became teachers and architects of what was taught. Some wanted professionals in the classrooms with professional curricular materials. In the end this new conception of parent involvement was accepted and eventually saved the program (Zigler & Muenchow, 1992). This parent control and participation has continued to keep the program grounded in the values and beliefs of the home communities. Unfortunately, the effects of this involvement have not been very well documented over the years but many attribute the major success of children in Head Start, not to the early intervention program *per se*, but to the strong involvement of families within the program.

The Abecedarian program did not have a strong parent involvement component. It was a program where the curriculum was devised by professionals and the staff was composed of adults from the minority community and other highly trained professionals. The lack of strong parent involvement hindered the complete success of the program, as many of us saw it. We were fortunate to have some of the respected leaders of the Black community on our staff, who were committed to our children. People like Carrie Bynum, who worked at the Frank Porter Graham Child Development Center guiding the intervention efforts, made our program credible to the Black community and her involvement with the children over the years clearly made a difference in the success of our children and in their continued participation in our program.

Apprenticeship and Mentoring

Although the major thrust of parent involvement in school may be to involve parents in decision-making within the school, there is another way to involve parents and other adults directly in student learning. This involvement can have a large impact on the success of individual children, regardless of the support of the administration and teachers. This is the concept of mentoring and apprenticeship in learning that has been mentioned before as a way that both the Mainstream and the Abecedarian children gained new skills in the neighborhood environment out of school.

Many of the skills that we learn for living are acquired out of school in culturally valued activities where competent adults and children participate with novices in activities that create competence in the novice without the fear of failure. Rogoff (1990) calls this apprenticeship in learning. It is seen in such formal activities as Boy Scouts and Girl Scouts and in everyday activities like cooking and gardening. Children in both the mainstream and minority families learn valuable skills by participating in these activities. In so doing they gradually become competent as the adult guides their participation toward competence without the judgment of failure or lack of ability.

Apprenticeship can also happen in our schools. Many research studies have shown that cross-age tutoring in schools benefits not only the novice but the expert as well. Community adults in classrooms have always been seen as beneficial to children of all ages. A book by Marc Freedman (1993), *The kindness of strangers*, details the mentoring movement, especially in our cities, of adult volunteers helping urban youth. A number of civic organizations and companies have set up mentoring programs for youth. In these programs not only are skills acquired in a successful way but adult modeling of success is experienced by the children themselves. The pairing of inner-city Black youths with successful Black businessmen produces youth who see success as possible and see that there is someone who may help them gain that success.

According to Freedman there are five reasons that mentoring works as a culturally accepted form of interaction by adults with children. First, it is *simple*. He means by this that it is easy to conceive and to practice since it involves one adult and one child. It personalizes the act of volunteering one's time. Second, it is *direct*. Mentors interact directly with the child. They are not removed from the real process but are intimately connected to it. Third, mentoring is *sympathetic*. Within our culture a mentor is seen as a positive and kind person and not as neutral as a tutor or volunteer. Fourth, mentoring is seen as *legitimate*. It is a sanctioned role within the society. Freedman attributes much of the present legitimacy of mentoring to the high profile and success of the Big Brothers/Big Sisters program. Last, mentoring is *bounded*. Even if mentors are committed and involved with the children they are not usurping the role of the parent or friend. There are emotional limits to mentoring that help both the child and the mentor define the parameters around their relationship.

This concept of mentoring can be used in the schools in an apprenticeship mode where older children can be mentors for younger ones and where competencies related to school can be accomplished in a more culturally acceptable style. This kind of teaching/learning was seen quite frequently in the neighborhoods of the Abecedarian children. It was often the case that older siblings and friends were the teachers of valued cultural skills for our children. The complex talk and teaching in the neighborhoods was not used in the school setting but it would seem easy to incorporate this apprenticeship concept into the teaching process.

In Conclusion

In many ways this book has painted a rather dismal picture of the transition to school for the African American children in the Abecedarian project. In other ways the study also painted an optimistic picture of the communities and families of these children. In spite of some unjustified assumptions about the deficits of the children and families made in the Abecedarian early intervention program, those children in early intervention did better in school on a number of dimensions compared to the non-intervention children. Yet, we have far to go if our goal is to make all or most of the Abecedarian children in our study and around the world succeed in school like most of the Mainstream children. Both groups of Abecedarian children were falling further behind their Mainstream peers as they progressed through elementary school.

Almost all children came to school ready to learn and we had only to be ready for them. It will be the challenge in the coming century for educators to be ready to teach all children, especially when most will be non-Caucasian and/or living below the poverty level. Without severe restructuring of Western society, schools are still the last great hope for the "good life" for children living in poverty. The creation of successful schooling for all children can happen if we are willing to give up some of the myths of the past and create new truths for the future.

References

Adler, M. (1988). *Reforming education: The opening of the American mind.* New York: Macmillan.

Alexander, K., & Entwisle, D. (1988). *Achievement in the first 2 years of school: Patterns and processes.* Chicago: University of Chicago Press.

Alexander, K. L., Entwisle, D. R., & Dauber, S. L. (1993). First-grade classroom behavior: Its short- and long-term consequences for school performance. *Child Development, 64,* 801–814.

Allen, W. R., Spencer, M. B., & Brookins, G. K. (1985). Synthesis: Black children keep on growing. In M. B. Spencer, G. K. Brookins, & W. R. Allen (Eds.), *Beginnings: The social and affective development of black children* (pp. 301–314). Hillsdale, NJ: Erlbaum.

Barker, R. G. (Ed.). (1963). *The stream of behavior.* New York: Appleton-Century-Crofts.

Bereiter, C., & Engelmann, S. (1966). *Teaching disadvantaged children in the preschool.* Englewood Cliffs, NJ: Prentice-Hall.

Bernstein, B. (1961). Social structure, language and learning. *Educational Research, 3,* 163–178.

Bernstein, B. (1966). Elaborated and restricted codes: Their social origins and some consequences. *American Anthropologist, 66* (No. 6, part 2).

Bernstein, B. (1971). Language and socialization. In N. Minnis (Ed.), *Linguistics at large* (pp. 227–245). New York: Viking.

Blank, M. (1975). Mastering the intangible through language. In I. D. Aaronson & R. W. Rieber (Eds.), *Developmental psycholinguistics and communication of sciences.* New York: New York Academy of Sciences.

Blank, M. (1982). Language and school failure: Some speculations about the relationship between oral and written language. In L. Feagans & D. C. Farran (Eds.), *The language of children reared in poverty* (pp. 75–93). New York: Academic Press.

Blank, M., Rose, S. A., & Berlin, L. J. (1978). *The language of learning: The preschool years.* New York: Grune & Stratton.

Bloom, B. S. (1964). *Stability and change in human characteristics.* New York: Wiley.

Bradley, L., & Bryant, P. (1985). *Rhyme and reason in reading and spelling.* Ann Arbor: University of Michigan Press.

Bronfenbrenner, U. (1979). *The ecology of human development.* Cambridge, MA: Harvard University Press.

Cairns, R. B. (1979). *Social development: The origins and plasticity of interchanges.* San Francisco: Freeman.

Caldwell, B. M. (1968). The fourth dimension in early childhood education. In R. D. Hess & R. M. Bear (Eds.), *Early education: Current research and action* (pp. 71–81). Chicago: Aldine.

Campbell, F. A. (1991, April). The Carolina Abecedarian Project. In M. R. Burchinal (Chair), *Early experience and children's competencies: New findings from four longitudinal studies.* Symposium conducted at the Biennial Meeting of the Society for Research on Child Development, Seattle, WA.

Campbell, F., & Ramey, C. (1994). Effects of early intervention on intellectual and academic achievement: A follow-up study of children from low-income families. *Child Development, 2,* 684–698.

Carnegie Council on Adolescent Development (1989). *Turning points: Preparing American youth for the 21st century.* New York: Carnegie Corporation of New York.

Cheatham, H. E. (1991). Empowering Black families. In H. E. Cheatham & J. B. Stewart (Eds.), *Black families: Interdisciplinary perspectives* (pp. 373–393). New Brunswick, NJ: Transaction Publishers.

Cheatham, H. E., & Stewart, J. B. (Eds.). (1991). *Black families: Interdisciplinary perspectives.* New Brunswick, NJ: Transaction Publishers.

Comer, J. (1985). The Yale-New Haven primary prevention project: A follow-up. *Journal of the American Academy of Child Psychiatry, 24,* 154–160.

Comer, J. (1992). Preface: A growing crisis in youth development. In *A matter of time: Risk and opportunity in the nonschool hours.* Report of the Task Force on Youth Development and Community Programs. New York: Carnegie Corporation.

Committee for Economic Development (1991). *The unfinished agenda: A new vision for child development and education.* New York: Committee for Economic Development.

Courlander, H. (1963). *Negro Folk Music, USA.* New York: Columbia University Press.

Davies, A. (Ed.). (1977). *Language and learning in early childhood.* London: Heinemann.

Davis, E. E. (1977). *My friends and me.* Circle Pines, MN: American Guidance Service.

Deutsch, M., Katz, D., & Jensen, A. R. (1968). *Social class, race, and psychological development.* New York: Holt, Rinehart and Winston.

Donaldson, M. (1978). *Children's minds.* London: Fontana.

Doughty, P., Thornton, G., & Doughty, A. (1977). *Language study: The school and the community.* New York: Elsevier.

Dunn, J. (1985). *Sisters and brothers.* Cambridge, MA: Harvard University Press.

Dunn, J. (1988). *The beginnings of social understanding.* Cambridge, MA: Harvard University Press.

Dunn, J., & Kendrick, C. (1982). *Siblings: Love, envy, and understanding.* New York: Cambridge University Press.

Dunn, L. M., Chun, L. T., Crowell, D. C., Dunn, L. G., Avery, L. G., & Yachel, E. R. (1976). *Peabody early education kit.* Circle Pines, MN: American Guidance Service.

Elder, G. H., Jr. (1974). *Children of the Great Depression.* Chicago: University of Chicago Press.

Elder, G. H., Jr. (1979). Historical change in life patterns and personality. In P. B. Baltes & O. G. Brim, Jr. (Eds.), *Life span development and behavior* (Vol. 2). New York: Academic Press.

Elder, G. H., Jr. & Rockwell, R. C. (1978). Economic depression and post-war opportunity in men's lives: A study of life patterns and health. In R. A. Simmons (Ed.), *Research in community and mental health* (pp. 240–303). Greenwich, CT: JAI Press.

Entwisle, D. R., & Alexander, K. L. (1990). Beginning school math competence. *Child Development, 61,* 454–471.

Entwisle, D. R., Alexander, K. L., Cadigan, D., & Pallas, A. M. (1987). Kindergarten experience: Cognitive effects or socialization? *American Educational Research Journal, 24,* 337–364.

Farran, D. C. (1990). Effects of intervention with disadvantaged and disabled children: A decade review. In S. J. Meisels & J. P. Shonkoff (Eds.), *Handbook of early childhood intervention* (501–539). New York: Cambridge University Press.

Farran, D. C., Burchinal, P., East, S., & Ramey, C. T. (1978, April). *Attachment between daycare infants and their teachers.* Paper presented at the Southeastern Conference on Human Development, Atlanta.

Farran, D. C., & Haskins, R. (1980). Reciprocal influence in the social interactions of mothers and 3-year-old children from different socioeconomic backgrounds. *Child Development, 51,* 780–791.

Feagans, L., & Appelbaum, M. I. (1986). Validation of language subtypes in learning disabled children. *Journal of Educational Psychology, 78,* 358–364.

Feagans, L., & Farran, D. (1981). How demonstrated comprehension can get muddled in production. *Developmental Psychology, 17,* 718–727.

Feagans, L., & Farran, D. C. (Eds.). (1982). *The language of children reared in poverty: Implications for evaluation and intervention.* New York: Academic Press.

Feagans, L. V., & Farran, D. C. (1994). The effects of day care intervention in the preschool years on the narrative skills of poverty children in kindergarten. *International Journal of Behavioral Development, 17,* 503–523.

Feagans, L. V., Fendt, K., & Farran, D. C. (1995). the effects of day care intervention on teacher's ratings of the elementary school discourse skills in disadvantaged children. *International Journal of Behavioral Development, 18,* 243–261.

Feagans, L., & Fendt, K. (1991). The effects of intervention and social class on children's answers to concrete and abstract questions. *Journal of Applied Developmental Psychology, 12,* 115–130.

Feagans, L. V., & Haskins, R. (1986). Neighborhood dialogues of black and white 5-year-olds. *Journal of Applied Developmental Psychology, 7,* 181–200.

Feagans, L., & Short, E. J. (1984). Developmental differences in the comprehension and production of narratives by reading disabled and normally achieving children. *Child Development, 55,* 1727–1736.

Freedman, M. (1993). *The kindness of strangers: Adult mentors, urban youth, and the new voluntarism.* San Francisco: Jossey-Bass.

Gesell, A., & Amatruda, C. S. (1947). *Developmental diagnosis.* New York: Hoeber.

Gleason, J. B., & Perlman, R. Y. (1984). Acquiring social variation in speech. In R. Sinclair & H. Giles (Eds.), *Recent advances in language, communication, and social psychology.* Hillsdale, NJ: Erlbaum.

Gomes, P. J. (1993). The least of these. In A. S. Hoots (Ed.), *Prophetic voices: Black preachers speak on behalf of children* (pp. 28–29). Washington, DC: Children's Defense Fund.

Goodlad, J. I. (1984). *A place called school: Prospects for the future.* New York: McGraw-Hill.

Gordon, A. M. (1984). Adequacy of responses given by low-income kindergarten children in structured adult–child conversations. *Developmental Psychology, 20,* 881–892.

Gough, K. (1989). The origin of the family. In A. S. Skolnick & J. H. Skolnick (Eds.), *Family in transition* (pp. 22–39). Boston: Scott, Foresman.

Gray, S. W., & Klaus, R. A. (1968). The early training project and its general rationale. In R. D. Hess & R. M. Bear (Eds.), *Early education: Current theory, research and action* (pp. 63–70). Chicago: Aldine.

Greenberg, P., & Epstein, B. (1973). *Bridges to reading.* Morristown, NJ: General Learning Corporation.

Hamburg, D. A. (1992). *Today's children: Creating a future for a generation in crisis.* New York: Times Books.

Haskins, R. (1988). Child support: A father's view. In A. J. Kahn & S. B. Kamerman (Eds.), *Child support: From debt collection to social policy* (pp. 306–327). Beverly Hills, CA: Sage.

Haskins, R., Walden, T., & Ramey, C. T. (1983). Teacher and student behavior in high- and low-ability groups. *Journal of Educational Psychology, 75,* 865–876.

Heath, S. B. (1983). *Ways with words.* Cambridge: Cambridge University Press.

Herrnstein, R. J., & Murray, C. (1994). *The bell curve: Intelligence and class structure in American life.* New York: The Free Press.

Hess, R. D., & Shipman, V. C. (1965). Early experience and the socialization of cognitive modes in children. *Child Development, 36,* 869–886.

Hess, R. D., & Shipman, V. C. (1967). Cognitive elements in maternal behavior. In J. P. Hill (Ed.), *Minnesota symposia on child psychology.* Minneapolis: University of Minnesota Press.

Hill, R. B. (1991). Economic forces, structural discrimination, and Black family instability. In H. E. Cheatham & J. B. Stewart (Eds.), Black families: Interdisciplinary perspectives (pp. 87–105). New Brunswick, NJ: Transaction Publishers.

Hoots, A. S. (Ed.). (1993). *Prophetic voices: Black preachers speak on behalf of children.* Washington, DC: Children's Defense Fund.

Hunt, J. (1961). *Intelligence and experience.* New York: Ronald Press.

Jensen, A. R. (1969). How much can we boost IQ and scholastic achievement? *Harvard Educational Review, 30,* 1–123.

Johnson, L. B. (1965). *The New York Times,* p. 90.

Kagan, J. S. (1969). Inadequate evidence and illogical conclusions. *Harvard Educational Review, 30,* 126–129.

Kellam, S. G., Ensminger, M. E., & Turner, R. J. (1977). Family structure and the mental health of children. *Archives of General Psychiatry, 34,* 1012–1022.

Kotlowitz, A. (1991). *There are no children here.* New York: Doubleday.

Labov, W. (1969). The logic of non-standard English. In P. P. Giglioli (Ed.) (1972), *Language and social context.* Harmondsworth: Penguin Books.

Labov, W. (1970). The logic of nonstandard English. In F. Williams (Ed.), *Language and poverty: Perspectives on a theme.* Chicago: Markham.

Labov, W. (1972). *Language in the inner city: Studies in the Black English Vernacular.* Philadelphia: University of Pennsylvania Press.

Lazar, I., Darlington, R., Murray, H., Royce, J., & Snipper, A. (1982). Lasting effects of early education: A report from the Consortium for Longitudinal Studies. *Monographs of the Society for Research in Child Development, 47* (2–3, Serial No. 195).

Lerner, R. M. (1984). *On the nature of human plasticity.* New York: Cambridge University Press.

Lerner, R. M. (1986). *Concepts and theories of human development* (2nd ed.). New York: Random House.

Lewis, C. C. (1984). Cooperation and control in Japanese nursery schools. *Comparative Education Review,* Feb., 69–84.

Linney, J. A., & Seidman, E. (1989). The future of schooling. *American Psychologist, 44,* 336–340.

Martin, S. L., Ramey, C. T., & Ramey, S. L. (1990). The prevention of intellectual impairment in children of impoverished families: Findings of a randomized trial of educational daycare. *American Journal of Public Health, 80,* 844–847.

McGinness, G. D. (1982). The language of the poverty child: Implications for intervention and evaluation derived from center based programs. In L. Feagans & D. C. Farran (Eds.), *The language of children reared in poverty* (pp. 219–240). New York: Academic Press.

McGinness, G., & Ramey, C. T. (1981). Developing sociolinguistic competence in children. *Canadian Journal of Early Childhood Education, 1,* 22–43.

National Commission on Children (1991). *Beyond rhetoric: A new American agenda for children and families*. Washington, DC: National Commission on Children.

Natriello, G., McDill, E. L., & Pallas, A. M. (1990). *Schooling disadvantaged children: Racing against catastrophe*. New York: Teachers College Press.

Nightingale, C. H. (1993). *On the edge: A history of poor Black children and their American dreams*. New York: Basic Books.

Ninio, A. (1980). Picture book reading in mother–infant dyads belonging to two subgroups in Israel. *Child Development, 51*, 587–590.

Ninio, A. (1989). The roots of narratives: Discussing recent events with very young children. *Language Sciences, 10*, 22–30.

Ochs, E., & Schieffelin, B. B. (Eds.). (1979). *Developmental pragmatics*. New York: Academic Press.

Ochs, E., & Schieffelin, B. B. (1984). Language acquisition and socialization: Three developmental stories and their implications. In R. Schweder & R. LeVine (Eds.), *Culture and its acquisition*. Chicago: University of Chicago Press.

Ogbu, J. U. (1982). Societal forces as a context of ghetto children's school failure. In L. Feagans & D. C. Farran (Eds.), *The language of children reared in poverty* (pp. 117–138). New York: Academic Press.

Ogbu, J. U. (1985). A cultural ecology of competence among inner-city blacks. In M. B. Spencer, G. K. Brookins, & W. R. Allen (Eds.), *Beginnings: The social and affective development of black children* (pp. 45–66). Hillsdale, NJ: Erlbaum.

Ogbu, J. (1988). Cultural diversity and human development. *New Directions for Child Development, 42*, 11.

Ogbu, J. U. (1991). Minority status and literacy in comparative perspective. In S. R. Graubord (Ed.), *Literacy* (pp. 141–168). New York: Hill and Wang.

Piaget, J. (1926). *The language and thought of the child*. New York: Harcourt, Brace and Brace.

Poole, T. G. (1991). Black families and the Black church: A sociohistorical perspective. In H. E. Cheatham & J. B. Stewart (Eds.), *Black families* (pp. 33–48). New Brunswick, NJ: Transaction Publishers.

Ramey, C. T., & Campbell, F. A. (1979). Early childhood education for psychosocially disadvantaged children: The effects of psychological processes. *American Journal of Mental Deficiency, 83*, 645–648.

Ramey, C. T., & Campbell, F. A. (1984). Preventive education for high-risk children: Cognitive consequences of the Carolina Abecedarian Project. *American Journal of Mental Deficiency, 88,* 515–523.

Ramey, C. T., & Campbell, F. A. (1991). Poverty, early childhood education, and academic competence: The Abecedarian experiment. In A. Huston (Ed.), *Children in poverty* (pp. 190–221). New York: Cambridge University Press.

Ramey, C. T., & Haskins, R. (1981). The causes and treatment of school failure: Insights from the Carolina Abecedarian Project. In M. Begab (Ed.), *Psychosocial influences and retarded performance: Strategies for improving social competence* (Vol. 2, pp. 89–112). Baltimore: University Park Press.

Ramey, C. T., McGinness, G., Cross, L., Collier, A., & Barrie-Blackley, S. (1982). The Abecedarian approach to social competence: Cognitive and linguistic intervention for disadvantaged preschoolers. In K. Borman (Ed.), *The social life of children in a changing society* (pp. 145–174). Hillsdale, NJ: Erlbaum.

Ramey, C. T., & Smith, B. (1977). Assessing the intellectual consequences of early intervention with high-risk infants. *American Journal of Mental Deficiency, 81,* 318–324.

Raph, J. B. (1965). Language development in socially disadvantaged children. *Review of Educational Research, 35,* 389–400.

Rogoff, B. (1990). *Apprenticeship in thinking: Cognitive development in social context.* New York: Oxford University Press.

Rogoff, B. (1993). Children's guided participation and participatory appropriation in sociocultural activity. In R. H. Wozniak & K. W. Fischer (Eds.), *Development in context: Acting and thinking in specific environments.* Hillsdale, NJ: Erlbaum.

Rutter, M., Yule, B., Morton, J., & Bagley, C. (1975). Children of West Indian immigrants – III: Home circumstances and family patterns. *Journal of Child Psychology and Psychiatry, 16,* 105–123.

Schieffelin, B. B. (1979). Getting it together: An ethnographic approach to the study of the development of communicative competence. In E. Ochs & B. B. Schieffelin (Eds.), *Developmental pragmatics.* New York: Academic Press.

Sinclair, J. McH., & Coulthard, R. M. (1975). *Towards an analysis of discourse.* Oxford: Oxford University Press.

Snow, C. E., Barnes, W. S., Chandler, J., Goodman, I. F., & Hemphill, L. (1991). *Unfulfilled expectations: Home and school influences on literacy.* New York: Cambridge University Press.

Sparling, J., & Lewis, I. (1979). *Learning games for the first three years*. New York: Walker Educational Book Corporation.

Spencer, M. B. (1985). Cultural cognition and social cognition as identity correlates of black children's personal-social development. In M. B. Spencer, G. K. Brookins, & W. R. Allen (Eds.), *Beginnings: The social and affective development of black children*. Hillsdale, NJ: Erlbaum.

Spencer, M. B., Brookins, G. K., & Allen, W. R. (Eds.). (1985). *Beginnings: The social and affective development of black children*. Hillsdale, NJ: Erlbaum.

Stack, C. B. (1974). *All our kin: Strategies for survival in a black urban community*. New York: Harper and Row.

Staples, B. (1994). Into the white ivory tower. *The New York Times Magazine*, February 6, pp. 22–26 and 36.

Steele, C. M. (1992). Race and the schooling of Black Americans. *The Atlantic Monthly*, April, 68–78.

Sutton-Smith, B., & Roberts, J. M. (1981). Play games and sports. In H. C. Triandis & A. Heran (Eds.), *Handbook of cross-cultural psychology* (Vol. 4). Boston, MA: Allyn and Bacon.

Tizard, B., Blatchford, P., Burke, J., Farquhar, C., & Plewis, I. (1988). *Young children at school in the inner city*. Hillsdale, NJ: Erlbaum.

Tizard, B., & Hughes, M. (1984). *Young children learning*. Cambridge, MA: Harvard University Press.

Tough, J. (1976). *Listening to children talking: A guide to the appraisal of children's use of language*. London: Ward Lock Educational Ltd.

Tough, J. (1977). Children and programmes: How shall we educate the young child? In A. Davies (Ed.), *Language and learning in early childhood*. London: Heinemann.

Tough, J. (1982). Language, poverty, and disadvantage in school. In L. Feagans & D. C. Farran (Eds.), *The language of children reared in poverty* (pp. 3–18). New York: Academic Press.

Valsiner, J. (1989). *Human development and culture*. Lexington, MA: Lexington Books.

Vygotsky, L. S. (1978). *Mind in society: The development of higher psychological processes*. Cambridge, MA: Harvard University Press.

Wallach, M. A., & Wallach, L. (1976). *Teaching all children to read*. Chicago: University of Chicago Press.

Ward, M. C. (1971). *Them children: A study in language learning*. New York: Holt, Rinehart and Winston.

Wechsler, D. (1967). *Wechsler Preschool and Primary Scale of Intelligence*. New York: The Psychological Corporation.

Weikert, D. P., Roger, L., Adcock, C., & McClelland, D. (1971). *The cognitively oriented curriculum.* Urbana, IL: University of Illinois Press.

Wells, G. (1981). *Learning through interaction: The study of language development.* New York: Cambridge University Press.

Wells, G. (1985). Preschool literacy-related activities and success in school. In D. R. Olsen, N. Torrance, & A. Hildyard (Eds.), *Literacy, language, and learning* (pp. 229–255). New York: Cambridge University Press.

Westinghouse Learning Corporation (1969). *The impact of Head Start: An evaluation of the effects of Head Start experience on children's cognitive and affective development* (preliminary draft). Columbus: Westinghouse Learning Corporation, Ohio University.

Wright Edelman, M. (1992). Preface. In D. A. Hamburg, *Today's children: Creating a future for a generation in crisis.* New York: Times Books.

Zigler, E., & Muenchow, S. (1992). *Head Start: The inside story of America's most successful educational experiment.* New York: Basic Books.

Index